C000151433

£1

Notes on Nationalism

Notes on Nationalism

Ramón Masnou Boixeda
Bishop Emeritus of Vic

Foreword by Doctor Narcís Jubany

GRACEWING

This work was first published in Catalan under the title
Carta Sobre Nacionalismes in April 1996 by
Edicions Proa, S.A., Barcelona

First published in Spanish under the title
Carta Sobre Nacionalismos in September 1996 by
Ediciones Península, S.A., Barcelona

First published in English in 2002

Gracewing
2 Southern Avenue, Leominster
Herefordshire HR6 0QF

ISBN 0 85244 561 X

Typeset by Action Publishing Technology Ltd,
Gloucester GL1 5SR

Printed by Antony Rowe Ltd.,
Chippenham, Wiltshire SN14 6LH

CONTENTS

FOREWORD

Monsignor Ramón Masnou, Bishop Emeritus of Vic, has kindly invited me to write the foreword for this book, modestly entitled *Notes on Nationalism*. Friends and brothers in the same episcopate, we have both been involved in pastoral work in Catalonia over many years: he in the diocese of Vic and I in the archbishopric of Barcelona. It is with considerable gratitude and great affection that I am writing this foreword to a work that scarcely needs introduction, dealing as it does with such a major, topical subject as that of nationalist philosophies.

Naturally Monsignor Masnou, as he himself declares in his introduction, has been concerned about the question of nationalist philosophies since his youth. In addition to the events he witnessed in Rome, while studying there in 1929, he has experienced many others since then, up to the present day. Obviously these memorable episodes have enriched his restless spirit – both wise and reflective – in the course of his long life as the priest and Bishop of Vic. The subject of nationalism in Catalonia has always, with good reason, interested him: it is undeniably relevant and indisputably present in the pastoral work of all Catalan dioceses. In 1986, conscious of this issue, the bishops of Catalonia published a joint pastoral instruction entitled *Arrels cristianes de Catalunya* (The Christian Roots of Catalonia), which recognised the identity of the Catalan people and the need for the central state to refrain at all times from hindering the natural development of our people.

There is a further reason why Monsignor Masnou has lived

Catalan nationalism so intensely: the fact that, for many years, he occupied the same episcopal see held by the renowned Bishop Josep Torras i Bages. The writings and exemplary life of this bishop made him an extraordinary character. In his day, he was known, without the least exaggeration, as 'the holy father of modern times' and 'the great patriarch of today's Christian generations'. He is well known for having published *La tradició catalana. Estudi del valor ètic i racional del regionalisme català* (Catalan Tradition. A Study of the Ethical and Rational Value of Catalan Nationalism) before his consecration as bishop, and reprinted several times over the course of his episcopal ministry. In this highly-documented work, Bishop Torras i Bages defends the social, political and spiritual personality of Catalonia throughout its long history. Benedict XV, the Pope of Peace, who was acquainted with the writings of the Bishop of Vic, praised him for having skilfully entered the world of politics on a 'sure' footing and for being such a thorough exponent of the ethical and political philosophy of Catalonia.

The so-called 'Catalan case' has been a source of debate for many years now. Recently, tension has regrettably arisen in magazines, radio programmes, articles and political speeches; prejudices abound and heated emotions are evident. This has only clouded the issue, hindered reflection and forestalled calm, mutually respectful and constructive dialogue, explaining why Monsignor Masnou has felt it his duty to write on nationalism. This is in the form of a series of notes, as he prefers a clear, accessible style and would like his point of view to be under-stood by all. Nevertheless the content is profound, as befits a teacher who never abandons complexity in an attempt to reach all his students.

In a previous book, entitled *El problema català* (The Catalan Problem) (1983), Monsignor Masnou addressed the Catalans to help them reflect upon the subject of nationalities. Here, by way of these notes, he speaks to his Spanish-speaking brothers. The purpose of this work is to develop a modest dialogue by present-ing views, reasons and suggestions. He has kept any hint of dogmatism at bay and in no way attempts to engage in conflict or attack.

Significantly, the author has chosen to enrich his text with various documents obtained from the Magisterium of the Church. In fact, they are teachings that form the basis for the assertions presented in this book. The subject of nationalism is important in social and political life. An article recently published in a Barcelona newspaper declares, 'today, as was the case sixty years ago, understanding the "Catalan case" is the crucial test in assessing the strength of Spanish democratic culture.' The author adds, 'those who will not accept that Catalonia can be what the majority of its citizens wish it to be, deserve not even a narrow pass mark in this subject.'

In this context the speech given by Pope John Paul II to the Fiftieth General Assembly of the UN on 5 December 1995, is of vital importance. As a document it steadfastly and clearly lays down Church thought, born as it is of natural law. The Pope, understandably, laments the absence of any international agreement covering the rights of nations as a whole, in contrast to the declared rights of man. After all, in specific terms of everyday community life, the rights of man give rise to the rights of nations, and need to be analysed on the basis of anthropology, ethics and law.

Language and culture are decisive in the issue of differences between nationalities and they illustrate the 'original spiritual sovereignty' of a people. The world has to learn to live with diversity, the Pope has declared. This diversity arises from existing cultural differences, which many consider a threat to the unity of the state. We need to understand that the concept of nation does not necessarily lead to the idea of state, and we need to remember that the rejection or oppression of differences is equivalent to negating the freedom of others. Furthermore, there are fundamental affinities between different cultures: they are simply distinct approaches to the sense of personal existence. Differences, through respectful dialogue, should provide a well of profound insight into the mystery of human existence, where the need for sympathy and solidarity is not sidelined.

The author declares himself to be a Spaniard who respects and admires the national values of language and culture, etc., of the Castilian nation, and reminds the reader that he is a Catalan who would refute any accusation of being a separatist. He observes, with extraordinary clarity, that most likely in the twenty-first century 'the current concept of independence will have lost its basic connotations in favour of a macro-community where, with no loss to their personality, nations will rediscover a heightened sense of motivation and better structures for interrelating'.

However, on the question of nationalism there is a lack of clear thinking, free from heated passions or prejudice. These notes – as Monsignor Masnou rightly asserts – attempt to help the reader form clear, fair ideas. This much-called-for work is undoubtedly a useful, important and necessary one.

Cardinal Narcís Jubany
Barcelona
11 December 1995

INTRODUCTION

An Ordinary Citizen and Retired Bishop

It is a good idea, I think, to write some notes or modest reflections on a subject pertinent to our times, an important one that easily creates an air of unpleasantness: the subject of nationalism and nationalist philosophies. I shall attempt to shed some light on the subject, from the perspective of a person concerned with the common good, a Christian believer and retired bishop.

There are many situations where a bishop, as an ordinary person, can think, speak and act in the lay world; situations that are not strictly religious, but which, for some important ethical reason, in the name of the common good, make it valuable and perhaps necessary for him to think, speak or act. This in no way implies that the contribution of an ordinary citizen/bishop is either more valuable or holds greater weight than that of a person who is not a bishop. Here his assertions are only as valuable as the argument or line of reasoning itself, as with the arguments of any other person.

Furthermore, a bishop, even when retired – as I am – has a mission to preach Christ's gospel, to help believers follow the Lord using the means available to the Church, and to serve his fellow man in finding the path to salvation, which crystallises in eternal happiness. It is what he is there to do. However, pursuing a nationalist philosophy can be the root of moral virtue or moral evil, which either leads to God, the creator of mankind, rights and nations, or distances the individual from Him. My aim is to help, if possible, people who love their nation to understand their rights and duties, so that they may behave as children of God, instead of pursuing ideas or laws that are not good, only the criteria and whims of men who abuse or err in their ways.

I am Catalan

Another aspect of these reflections is that the person writing is not only a citizen and a Bishop Emeritus, but also a Catalan. It is an important factor in the issue under discussion. It would not be so relevant if I had been born in Castile or Andalusia, which deserve as much esteem and respect as Catalonia. The adjective 'important', used here, refers to the often recognised fact that in other lands in Spain, the expressions 'Catalonia' and 'Catalan' in many people arouses ideas, feelings, opinions, assertions, comments, behaviour and suspicions that the names of other lands in the peninsula do not. I say 'many people' because not everyone reacts strongly to the word 'Catalan' or is disturbed by it.

To those who may be taken aback by these notes on a subject that draws so much attention, written by an author who is both Catalan and a bishop, I am bound to say that I am not surprised by your reaction, nor am I upset by it. However, please do not be overquick to react, or feel slightly annoyed, dismissive or disinterested. Be kind and patient and continue reading in the knowledge that I have written this book, not from the position of an enemy trench, but with a thirst for dialogue and in good-will.

I Address Fellow Citizens in the Other Nations and Regions of Spain

Firstly, I should like to be more specific as to this book's intended audience. I address citizens – for me, brothers and sisters – in the other nations and regions of Spain. It presumably will not reach the hands of readers preoccupied with other pressing problems, especially those of a personal, family or social nature, a common thing in these busy, anxious times. Neither do I think it will be of interest to those fellow citizens who feel that they are already well informed, well read and sure of their opinions, convictions or standpoint, keep them intact and intangible, and are quite unprepared to hear opinions, reflections or suggestions which could, perhaps, enrich their knowledge if they were acquainted with them. As I mentioned before, I do wish it to reach those who are similarly open to dialogue and generously welcome my points of view, which are neither articles of faith, nor aggressive or impossible dreams, and later form an opinion as their conscience dictates. As for myself, during the course of my life I have learnt and read with peace and respect the opinions of many brothers with opposite convictions on this subject.

I consider all men to be my brothers, but I especially apply this endearment to all those baptised in the name of Christ who wish to live the social consequences of their Catholic faith. Why? The reason is simple and, at the same time, very important. Because as Catholics we should be the first to conduct and teach dialogue and demonstrate exemplary co-operation on the matter of nationalism.[1]

---

[1] In the document *Arrels cristianes de Catalunya* (The Christian Roots of Catalonia), published by the Bishops of Catalonia in 1986, we see this comment: 'We would like our Catholic brothers from other peoples in Spain to be the first to recognise and welcome these aspirations. In contrast, we Catalan Catholics would also have to be the first in opening up to their problems. Carles Cardó, in 1930, remarked on the important repercussions for peace in Spain if Catholics were to embark on the noble task of helping their fellow citizens understand problems experienced by others. He proposed conducting a round of self-criticism from the perspective of Catalonia and asked other Spaniards to let go of "the disastrous idea that confuses organic, unique, living unity with mechanical unity, which is always dead or about to die". But, as the distinguished thinker stressed, the painful paradox often arises that "those who do not have the light of faith show this Christian understanding and are ready for the glory, prestige and profit of its application. Many Catholics, in contrast, cling on stubbornly in impenetrable incomprehension"' (*La nit transparent* (The Transparent Night), published by La Paraula Cristiana, Barcelona, 1935, p. 181). This is a call for responsibility by Catholics which has not lost its relevance.

The Question of Nationalism has Concerned Me Since My Youth

I cannot hide the fact that I have been seriously interested in the subject since my days as a student, especially during the years I spent in Rome, at the height of Fascist rule. It coincided with the famous Lateran pact (1929), which resolved the so-called 'Roman question' between the Italian state and the Holy See and created what then became known as the Vatican City, along with its status as an independent state. My studies and prolonged stay with seminarists from all over Spain and other countries must have contributed something towards the formation of my ideas on nationalism. Of course I was much more influenced by the events and things I experienced and observed which, as I matured and above all took on episcopal responsibility, subsequently made their mark felt on me. The overwhelming statism of Italian Fascism, the horrors of Soviet totalitarianism, the genocidal racism of German National Socialism and other examples that were perhaps of lesser importance but equally worrying, made many of us reflect. Even Spain had its ups and downs. Suffice it to say, what few can claim, that I lived through the two political regimes of Primo de Rivera (1923–1930) and Franco (1939–1975). Not to mention the excesses of the Republic, or the terrible persecution in 1936 against everything religious, from which I escaped with my life – I won't say miraculously, as I was not destined by Divine Providence to bloodshed and martyrdom, but to live to a ripe old age, not without its crosses to bear.

There can be no doubt that all these events taught me lessons of which people today, mostly the young, have no experience and often do not, nor cannot, have any awareness. However, the most memorable event and the one that helped me the most to clarify my ideas was, without doubt, the Second Vatican Council (1962–1965) with its beautiful, assured documents which of course did not come from politicised or partisan sources, but from the serene vision of the hierarchical Magistracy of the Catholic Church. In contemporary times, this vision goes back, at least, to Leo XIII (see the encyclical *Libretas praestantissimum*), as Bishop Torres i Bages emphasised in *La tradició catalana* (Catalan Tradition), and continues with the teachings of Pius XI and Pius XII. The same was true of Pope

John XXIII (1958–1963), who sensed and prepared the Council, Paul VI (1962–1978) who led it to a happy conclusion, and Pope John Paul II who takes the opportunity, whenever it arises, to reiterate and develop the ideas of the Council in his writings and travels. It is well known that he has often spoken of nationalism, which shows that having fair, clear views on this question is not pointless, silly or just for excitable politicians, but something necessary and important.[2]

I have not been an obstinate preacher on the issue

As for myself, by writing these notes on nationalism for my Spanish-speaking brothers,[3] do not be misled into thinking I have been an obstinate preacher on this issue. In over 40 years of episcopal ministry, I have done no more than preach the gospel, speaking and writing at all times with absolute faith in the doctrine of the Church.

However, the fact that I have not been obsessed with the issue does not mean, as I just said, that I am indifferent to it. On the contrary, as it revolves heavily around humanism I have been forced to reflect as a Christian, a bishop and a citizen as and when circumstances have arisen. I shall simply refer to three pieces of writing that reflect, though in different ways, my ideas.

The first is the previously-mentioned document, *Arrels cristianes de Catalunya* (The Christian Roots of Catalonia), a joint work by the Episcopal Conference of Tarragona, to which I contributed as Bishop of Vic.

The second is a book entitled *El problema català* (The Catalan Problem) (1983), to guide those in search of information and clarification on the subject so that they may form an opinion and act accordingly. The book is written in Catalan and

---

[2]See documentation in Appendix One, pages 73–102 and 122–126.

[3]I will be using this term – 'Spanish-speaking brothers' – fairly frequently in order to not repeat the more exact term of 'the brothers of other nationalities and regions of Spain' which I have already used before. I am conscious of the linguistic and cultural richness present within the State: please do not think otherwise when I use the former – simpler – term. I am also aware that many citizens in Catalonia use this idiom, therefore please do not accuse me of forgetting this point, which is also essential. I trust that this explanation will prove sufficient to justify the use, to me transparent, of the said term.

addresses Catalans. When I wrote it I was free of my episcopal duties and attempting to put across my viewpoint on nationalism, especially Catalan nationalism, to the people of Catalonia – not from a political standpoint, but from an ethical and Christian one instead. This, I humbly believe, I achieved, without intending to be an authority or to exclude other views, obviously expounded with as much goodwill as my own.

The third is an article included in a book called *Miscellània Torras i Bages* (Torres i Bages Miscellany), published in 1991, on the seventy-fifth anniversary of the death of the venerable José Torres i Bages, saint and famous Bishop of the diocese of Vic, and author of *La tradició catalana*, an exemplary book in which he expounded and defended in depth his vision of the personality of Catalonia through history. Some of the works appearing in this volume, which I personally promoted, were written before 1966, in other words the fiftieth anniversary of the Bishop's death, but which were not published for various reasons.

Current Sources of Friction

Meanwhile, I have had a chance to learn about the deplorable friction there has been recently, and which unfortunately continues, in the media and politics against Catalonia and Catalans. It was just what I needed to convince myself of the importance of the subject and, above all, the value and need for the public and political parties to reflect on nationalism.

It seems reasons abound for me to write these pages, addressing my Spanish-speaking friends, as I once did years ago to my Catalan-speaking friends. I am not doing this for amusement, obsession or for political side-taking, but out of love for all my brothers, because considerable suffering has been caused by wrongly conceived nationalism – the current Pope, John Paul II, has called it exacerbated – and because it is my duty and wish to contribute to much-needed reflection upon the issue by way of thoughts and suggestions, without pontificating, and through unassuming dialogue so that conflict, attacks, harsh situations and verbal outbursts may be avoided. May the Lord help me succeed.

CHAPTER ONE

OUTLINE OF TYPES OF NATIONALISM

Nationalism as Love of Nation

From the outset, it is essential to state that nationalism, in terms of patriotism, love of and service to one's native land, is not wrong, though it may have certain defects like pride, vanity, disregard for others or chauvinism (the latter though no lover of service and sacrifice, is very capable of haranguing; its enthusiasm, however, is not matched by getting out its wallet). While on the subject, I have read that genuine Christian faith is expensive. The Christian, of course, must share his wealth with those poorer than himself, and many Christians pay lipservice to this but fail to do it. Today, the Third and Fourth Worlds are shameful testimony of this. Well, something similar happens, or so it seems, when it comes to many people's ideas of patriotism and nationalism.

Nationalism, as love of one's nation, when not marred by defect or devalued or discredited by abuse, injustice, violence, and war, is good. Christ loved his country, to the point of weeping for his beloved Jerusalem, which was about to suffer greatly for its sins. However, for a Christian, the most important thing is not to be a good nationalist, but to be a true disciple of Jesus, which, if he indeed is, will also make him a good patriot and lover of his nation.

And now I come to a thorny point, a burning prickly question which in theory should be easy, but in the world of facts and of opinions on facts tends to be quite complicated: that of the various kinds of nationalist philosophies – those that are clearly evil and those that are not. The Soviet and Nazi dictatorships are examples of clearly evil ones.

Criteria of Judgement

Any nationalist philosophy should be examined, judged, assessed and thought about with balanced objectivity which, more often than not, helps one understand its values and detriments. A balanced approach demands a serious, objective answer to two fundamental questions: is the nationalism in question aggressive? Or is it defensive? It stands to reason that these questions have to be answered seriously and objectively.

In some cases discerning judgement may not be easy, but in general I would say it is much easier for those who are not living with the problem, and that it would also be easy if those who were living it approached the problem with goodwill and an educated attitude, unemotionally and without prejudice, and showed an ability to draw the right conclusions after careful consideration. Real facts are valuable and important for a proper analysis, whereas animosity, utopias, vanity, ignorance and certain behaviour or propaganda in the media tend to be too negative to shed any light on an objective study whose aim is balanced judgement. A serious Christian who applies all the teachings of the gospel (being fair, humble, at peace, serene and capable of prayer), with the Lord's help, is capable of discerning judgement. One can and should depend more on God than on man.

Is it Good for Nationalism to Exist?

Some may wonder, is it good for nationalism to exist at all? I do not believe that this question can be answered with a simple yes or no. It would be good if nationalism did not exist and that none were needed. A love for one's country that is just, balanced and effective is enough, alongside love and respect for other nations. In particular, love and respect for the poorer countries in the Third World that lack food, medical care, education and all the needs to live as people at the beginning of the twenty-first century, forced to endure the cruel, indifferent gaze of many in the First World, who are greedy for pleasure, extravagance, luxury and all kinds of abuse involving money. In other words, if there were an abundance of justice and true love in the world, instead of so much injustice, immorality and wrongly employed money, nationalism would no longer be necessary.

However, the world is sick. There is a great deal of injustice between people, groups, nations and states. Instead of love and respect, very often throughout history and in our modern civilised times, the law of the fittest has been imposed on the weak. Instead of respecting the rights of others they abuse them and forget, meanwhile, their obligations. Big fish eats little fish, and lives and prospers in peace, because the fittest and the one with the most means, to defend and attack, is not loved but feared. This proves that there are forms of nationalism that are good and, to a greater or lesser extent, useful or necessary; not because you just happen to like it or out of wickedness, but to counter the influence of strong nations and states that do not honour the law of love and respect for the weakest.

Three Attitudes Towards Aggressive Nationalism

Absorption and abandonment

When the strong neither love nor respect and instead attack the weak (which, as we shall see, can take a variety of forms), the weak can counter this by adopting various attitudes: first, being patient, putting up with it, hiding, convincing oneself that the stronger party who is abusing and infringing rights is right and that, therefore, what the aggressor says and does is good.

Furthermore, it may be that the weak, or at least the frailest and most oppressed among them, reach precisely the situation that the strong, manipulating the former's rights, has been wanting. There are two stages to this: the first is that, over time, while continually abusing the means he has available to consolidate his position, the conqueror convinces the conquered that he is right, that this unjust situation is the best and only possible answer. The infringed rights of the weak no longer exist, there is no structure to defend them and they are not discussed, because the newly achieved status quo is untouchable and sacrosanct. So much so – and this is the second stage – that the weak oppressed group is also convinced of this change: their memory of the past is erased, they get used to the new state of affairs through education, laws and punishment and, over time, give in and submit to assimilation and uniformity. When this happens, the traditional rights of the weak are lost and the rights of the strong, the aggressor, are consolidated, so there are no longer two distinct groups, but one unified group.

Defence and armed struggle

The second attitude is the opposite and quite different: when the stronger group does not respect the weaker group, is troubled by it and uses harassment to depersonalise, assimilate and eradicate its individual, distinct, traditional values. It attempts to convert the weaker group into a vulgar submissive mass, subjecting them to the values of the dominant group by violence. The weak, however, are often not willing to accept the situation, are not resigned and call into action a plan of defence. It may start off with dialogue or diplomacy but, if this does not lead to positive results, ends in violence or war and, far from being short-lived, it is long and drawn-out and fraught with unforeseen complications.

It is an explicable and natural attitude, because the right to defend oneself is a human right shared by individuals and collectives alike. However, as a general rule, I think this attitude is ill-advised, inefficient and wrong, because violence does not tend to result in peace or justice. We know, only too well, that violence engenders violence, suffering and death. In other words, crushing one set of rights can be the cause of an endless list of further human rights abuses against innocent people. It does not seem logical to try to cure one wrong by committing further and worse wrongs. The current cases of Bosnia, Rwanda, etc. are instructive in so far as they demonstrate the consequences of violence as the wrong solution or response, even when the circumstances are very different.

Seen through Christian eyes, it seems more reasonable to live, do good and live a life of devotion within a climate of unjust submission with the concomitant loss of rights and just values (which is very common these days), rather than choosing violence and the wicked life it brings, offering little chance to do good or to live righteously. Christ, the apostles and the saints are men of peace. Peace and respect for others are basic values. If only those who abuse the weak would adopt peace as the weak do, as is God's will, when other, non-violent, means are perhaps at hand and are just as effective over time. In saying this, I do not mean to prejudge the justness of armed defence as a last and extraordinary recourse. (See note 3 on page 25, below.)

Resistance by peaceful means

Let us move on to the third attitude. Here the group or nation with stronger material powers, such as number of inhabitants, land, army, money and other advantages, adopts the aggressive stance described above. This may be either violent using weapons, invasion, appropriation of space, etc., or second-order violence: non-inflammatory behaviour but still oppressing the rights of the weak, causing suffering and strife, and threatening good relations and coexistence.

In this form of nationalism, the weak group suffering the infringement of rights again does not accept the situation, whether recently created or an ancient burden stretching back over many generations. They disagree, because they are conscious of the injustice. They stand up for the rights of their members using the peaceful means available to them. These may include not slackening in their drive to recover lost rights, or explaining the history of the problem in depth, seriously, honestly and calmly, without impassioned speechmaking or agitation. Modern-day cases, among others, that include the self-liberation of the Baltic Countries and the path to independence taken by the Czech Republic and Slovakia are instructive on how it is possible to obtain eminently positive results, not by taking the road to violence, but by a settlement reached through dialogue and democracy.

It should be borne in mind that, in order to maintain its position, the stronger party has, to a greater or lesser extent, distorted history and fostered ignorance, slanting or covering up the facts, thereby ensuring that a considerable number of people are kept ignorant of the facts and lose interest in the subject.

In these difficult cases, it is important for the dominant group to realise that it, too, is a nationalist group or nation. This point is all important. It may, and often does, occur that it is the weak group, trying to defend the infringement of its human rights and characteristics that make up the so-called national differential factor, who are singled out and accused of or said to be nationalist, in the pejorative sense of the word. In reality it is the group infringing the rights of the weak who is the most markedly nationalist – it simply employs a different type of nationalism that goes under another name.

Indeed, there is one type of nationalism that defends itself, as any individual experiencing the infringement of his rights will defend himself, and another that is aggressive and is the real cause of the problem or conflict, although the latter is not pleased by the term. When the rights of people are infringed, the term for measured response is called defensive. Likewise, groups or nations whose attitude or action violates rights are, rightly, called aggressive. Whether the reader likes it or not, the division of the concept of nationalism into two types, aggressive and defensive, is a fact. When the Islamic armies invaded the peninsula, nobody disputes that their behaviour was aggressive and that, if the attempt to transform the Visigoth kingdom into a Muslim Caliphate had proved successful, it would have been a clear case of expansive aggression and those attacked, by resisting, would have offered a clear example of a defensive position. In the end, the long-term objective was never achieved and various mediaeval kingdoms arose. The same, I suppose, may be said of the French invasion of Spain by Napoleon.

What is open to debate is whether aggression is present or not in each example of nationalism, to what degree and how it may be proved, a point which should be demonstrated not on the basis of words, be they of enthusiasm or resentment, but with facts. In the various theories on nationalist philosophies discussed here, we need to clarify and search for the truth, something which, as I have said, cannot be done through violence, whether first- or second-degree, but through study and dialogue by experts (historians, lawyers, thinkers, writers, journalists, political parties, etc.) on both sides. This is something that requires tranquillity and peace of mind, not conflict and statements of little value or poor taste, or within a climate of restricted freedoms.

The Purpose of These Notes

It is my intention here to pen some notes on nationalist philosophies, precisely when certain clouds have let fall such a torrent of inappropriate, unjustified, offensive and regrettable claims. The ordinary people of Catalonia do not understand what has set off so much unfriendliness and lack of constructive common sense from those perpetrating these ideas. These notes of mine are not aimed along these lines. They are written precisely so that things like this do not happen again, so that those who think like this, instead of bursting out in rage, reason things through and analyse in depth – with sincerity, proper documentation and respect – the reasons and motives for their position. I have always admired the greatness, in all senses, granted to the Spanish-speaking lands of Spain by Providence. Catalonia has neither attempted, nor sought, to destroy the traditional wealth and characteristics of the Spanish-speaking nation, much less has it attempted to destroy the Spanish tongue, assured of expansion and its place throughout so many countries of the Americas.

CHAPTER TWO

THE ANTI-CATALAN SYNDROME

The Age of Attacking Catalonia

The climate of disagreeable animosity towards Catalonia and everything Catalan that has persisted since its distant origins, sometimes less intensely so, and other times taking a more severe, inflammatory turn, is a state of affairs which needs to completely disappear and be replaced with a climate of understanding and respect. It is a phenomenon that has caused many problems and much suffering, and constantly threatens further severe situations, with the associated danger of political consequences, changes or disruption. The problem is not one solely affecting Catalans, but also those who are not. It is a problem that, despite the measures taken to date, has yet to be resolved, though the situation may have improved for some.

The Problem Needs to be Faced

I believe that this is a problem that requires looking at carefully, to study and understand its components from a personal perspective and from the standpoint of the other individuals involved. It is a problem we cannot afford to shy away from, as has so often occurred in the past, where opinions have been expressed with so much certainty, finality and obstinacy, that the opinion of others has not merited a hearing or been listened to.

If relations between two individuals or groups in disagreement are conducted under these faulty conditions and we then add an absence of virtuous qualities such as patience, humility and love of one's fellow man, it becomes extremely difficult to find a reasonable, fair mid-point where it is possible to come to agreement. The path of dialogue will be cut off and the arguing and quarrelling will go on indefinitely. Over the course of many years, with democracies and dictatorships in between, and extremists from either side, I have had the opportunity to encounter and know some of the evil caused by ignorance, misunderstanding, injustice, animosity, enmity and so many other unhappy states. It has given me something resembling the right and duty to speak as a brother, not as a governor or politician, with the sole desire of helping my fellow man.

Why This Malaise?

I honestly wonder why there has been this evident, veritable malaise between one group of renowned, influential Spanish-speaking people and another group of also renowned, mostly Catalan-speaking people for three centuries now? It is a malaise that always emerges and manifests itself in a disagreeable manner, and has become more or less recognised as a reality throughout Spain and abroad. I say 'evident, veritable malaise', because there are plenty of people who claim that 'there's nothing going on', 'there's no problem', 'it's an obsession shared by a few individuals' and that 'it's all been resolved'. It is true that the arrival of democracy polished a few rough edges and there was some dialogue. Scores of other problems and the good manners shown by the general public gave a certain feeling of peace on this issue. But, suddenly, when least expected, the pot boiled up unpredictably when the subject of teaching Catalan in Catalonia was broached and also later when it came to the elections for the European Parliament. What came about was surprising, oppressive and sadly meaningful: thin ashes covered embers that refused to go out and flared up terribly at the merest gust of wind. The embers of the problem are still there and very much alive. I have no wish to recount history or describe what occurred, I only refer to recent events in that they are far from unique in what they demonstrate.

It is a fact that the anti-Catalan syndrome persists and, sadly and alarmingly, it is expressed by certain people, bodies and communications media. I have yet to see, or at least I do not remember seeing, any similar uproar aimed at any other people in Spain. Why have the two dictatorships I have known and lived through been so harsh towards Catalonia? I do not wish to go into detail naming events and giving examples of this harshness, as if I were outraged and listing grievances. The history of Catalonia covers the subject well enough and more than one book exclusively dedicated to this topic has been published in Catalonia. I have the feeling that, outside Catalonia, this aspect of history has been fundamentally ignored and I think, for basic realism, it would be beneficial and useful for it to be better known and understood, not in order to upset or polarise opinions, but to encourage reflection, meditation and understanding.

The Syndrome seen from Catalonia

This ingrained, widespread grudge held by so many Spanish-speaking people against everything Catalan, when seen from Catalonia by the ordinary Catalan, is inexplicable. It is considered endemic and inevitable: all one can do about it is to be patient and not worry about it too much.

From the point of view of the better informed, it is considered to be an enduring peculiarity that children inherit from their parents (passed down in turn from their parents); something that students learn from their teachers; something experienced in the barracks during military service; something inhaled from books, in literature, patriotic events, conversation; and which most think of as natural, logical and not in contradiction with ethics or religion.

The learned Catalan used to think that this climate had improved somewhat, perhaps due to certain factors such as, for example: that the new Constitution spoke without fear or hesitation about regional autonomies and nationalities; the highly tranquil coexistence enjoyed by the citizens of Catalonia, whether native or non-native, Spanish or Catalan speaking; the abundant availability of information in the social media; writers and thinkers from various backgrounds in the peninsula meeting together; increased contact between leaders, movement and institutions within the Church; the fact that many foreign universities now taught the Catalan tongue abroad; the significant fact that, within the doctrine of the Catholic Church, the teachings of the Second Vatican Council and the Magistracy of the Popes from John XXIII to John Paul II had continually spoken out in favour of the rights of nationalities and ethnic minorities, and against aggressive nationalism; the debate and promotion of the Europe of the Regions, etc. These things as seen by, as I say, the better educated, made the rancid forms of the anti-Catalan syndrome more difficult to see clearly. Unfortunately, these factors have not helped alleviate the old anti-Catalan tradition as much as had been hoped for, at least not among the more learned circles, where a more reasonable approach and a capacity to conduct serious, studious debate in goodwill, free of attack or insult, should have been expected.

The Goal of Information and Dialogue

So far I have written about the fact that an anti-Catalan syndrome does exist. I could go further into the topic, but it is a bitter subject and could upset some readers. The above was not a protest, accusation or an attempt to complicate matters. I have brought up this syndrome, because it is a subject worth investigating against the background of nationalist philosophies. My intention is highly objective and realistic: that as much as possible should be done through dialogue and sound information to make the anti-Catalan syndrome, a cause of ill will and suffering, gradually lose ground and, though it might seem difficult or even impossible to imagine, make it disappear entirely. A reasonable nationalist viewpoint might achieve this. And, deep down, this is the problem. There is a lack of ideas that are free of emotion and prejudice. I hope to God that the ill-informed may be receptive to some of these ideas, and that those who perhaps have not valued them sufficiently before may be reminded of their importance.

CHAPTER THREE

THE ISSUE IN DEPTH

A Clarification of Concepts: Nationalism, Nation, State

Nationalism

Definitions

What is nationalism? In order to continue in my style, not as a expert but a thinker, I will first quote two definitions of nationalism.

The first I transcribe from the *Diccionario ideológico de la lengua española* (Ideological Dictionary of the Spanish Language) by Julio Casares (second edition, updated [fourth run], Barcelona, 1959), 'Nationalism: The attachment shown by the natives of a nation to its habits and customs. Political doctrine which converts a more or less autonomous part of a nation or territory into a state.' 'The tendency to extol the personality of a nation' (p. 578).

I use and translate the second one from the *Diccionari de la Llengua Catalana* (Dictionary of the Catalan Language) (Fundació Enciclopèdia catalana, Barcelona, 1982), 'Nationalism: Political behaviour directly arising from the attribution, on ethical-political grounds, of a very high regard to the national factor or nation' (p. 1061).

Comments

I do not think these two definitions need much analysis. The term 'attachment to habits and customs' is clear. Each to his own. There is no problem, unless the attachment degenerates into contempt or ill-treatment of others. The same may be said about 'tendency to extol the personality of a nation'. If the act of extolling is reasonable, is not immoral and does not harm anyone, and lies within the bounds of common sense, it should not cause any problem. We need to be clear on the point where the definition states, 'Political doctrine which converts a more or less autonomous part of a nation or territory into a state'. In order for a part of a nation or territory to become a state, I do not think that doctrine is enough. Certain special circumstances must also exist which logically demand it as an objective and it must also include the will of the people living in the territory, whether all or a majority, to bring about this change justifiably on the basis of these special circumstances. The doctrine itself does not create the change or conversion, it is rather that the doctrine is justified by and based on these special circum-stances. It is not a question of capricious change.

The second definition, for the moment, I do not believe requires any special observation, except perhaps that an attitude which exalts the national factor or nation is not based on passing whim, but on very serious, valid factors or circumstances.

These definitions contain words such as 'more or less autonomous state', 'part of the nation', 'territory', 'nation', 'national factor', etc. The two most important concepts are 'nation' and 'state'. It would be a good idea to define both so that we can then reflect on them. Without clear ideas on nation and state, it is difficult to talk or think about nationalism.

Nation

Concept

The first dictionary says, 'Nation: Group of inhabitants in a country governed by the same government' (p. 578). As we can appreciate, this is a simple definition, too simple in my opinion; it states something that is true, but I do not believe that it consists of all the truth. We need to find a definition that is richer in content, more explicit. Looking, therefore, in the *Diccionari de la Llengua Catalana* we see the following, 'Nation: A community of individuals whose basically cultural but diversified ties, economic structure and common history, have given them a physiognomy of their own, with distinct and differentiating features, and a desire for autonomous government and influence which, taken to its limit, leads them to want to be endowed with their own political institutions to the point of constituting a state' (p. 1061).

Comments

The latter is a definition rich in the ingredients that make up the concept of 'nation'. You can see how it circumscribes the single idea of nation, of a nation that is not yet a state, but which could become one because it possesses the essential components of nations endowed with statehood. It only lacks the institutional levels that culminate in the structure of a state. The state is independent and sovereign. The nation is neither one thing nor the other, but it does have those elements that would constitute it as such: elements that have come together over time and history. This is not the result of the ideas and hopes of men or governments, who are not able to create them artificially in their full, complete sense, but has other causes, some explicable, others perhaps not so easily explained, all allowed by or subject to the mysterious ways of Divine Providence.

The creation of states is the work of men. States are constituted on the basis of one or sometimes more nations, which they subsequently manage with resources, uses and abuses, made possible by sovereignty and power. Basically what is often claimed is true: while states change and can be made and unmade through wars, treaties or lines on a sheet of paper (since government leaders, limited as they are by ignorance, have not always treated other peoples well), nations are more the result of general cultural sedimentation under the Providence of God, than the well-argued intentions of men.[1]

---

[1]The Magistracy is very insistent on the cultural or civilisation component. John Paul II, in his famous speech to UNESCO, predominantly stressed the cultural dimension of the concept of nation, 'In effect the nation is a large community of people united by a variety of ties but, above all, precisely by culture. The nation exists *"because of"* culture and *"for"* culture ...' (See page

State

Preliminaries

What I have just written may give a certain impression of prejudice against the institution of the state, in contrast to the entity of the nation. This is not so. I cherish a very positive notion of the state, as I do of other similar concepts, such as democracy. But I have a certain amount of difficulty when the concept crosses into real life. In the hands of men, with their limitations and faults, much of its value is lost, and the selfsame citizens and politicians whose errors and bad habits are to blame for its deterioration usually pay their tribute. In themselves, therefore, the idea of state and the idea of nation do not contradict one another when the opinions and deeds of men are logical and right.

Concept

The definitions of state given in the dictionaries that I have at hand are not very explicit or useful when it comes to examining the relationship between state and nation. Nevertheless, I will copy them out. The Casares dictionary: 'State: the political body of a nation' (p. 363). *Diccionari de la Llengua Catalana*: 'State: historical, social formation, organised as a political unit with its own characteristics' (p. 675).

---

73 and following pages in the Appendix of this book). Among the cultural elements, the most important one is language. In his speech to the young people of Tokyo (24 February 1981), John Paul II asserted, 'The culture of each nation is expressed, among other ways yet more than any other, in language. Language is the form we give to our thoughts, it is like a robe onto which we pin these thoughts. Language embraces the peculiar traits which give a people and a nation their identity. And, in some way, the heart of the nation lies latent within it, because language, one's own language, gives expression to what feeds man's soul in the community of a family, of a nation, of history.' Already Pius XII, in his Christmas message broadcast in 1954, declared that, 'national life is, in itself, the operating group of all those values of civilisation that belong to and are characteristic of a specific group, whose spiritual unity is constituted by a common tie'. Furthermore, he added that national life can develop in conjunction with other national lives within the same State (see note 3, Chapter Four).

Comments

A nation is a community of people endowed with special characteristics (not common, such as the dignity that God has granted
all men and women as His children, according to Christian revelation), characteristics that are values which enrich a community. These characteristics are not in opposition to those of other
communities – on the contrary, they mutually strengthen and
accompany each other through their history. If the individuals
that make up this community interweave personal and social
relationships, share needs and services, lean towards a common
good and benefit from this, it stands to reason that they need a
body to direct, order, foster, protect, command or prohibit all
that is needed for this common good to exist and so that its
members and beneficiaries may duly and fairly participate in it.
The body that this community-nation needs is the state. The state
is the guarantor of the common good of the nation, as much in
terms of the organisation of life inside the territory itself, as in the
relationships struck with fellow communities.

Rights and duties of the state

We should not forget that the state, despite all the power it
enjoys (and needs), and the growing resources it has at its
disposal, has no right, be it by God's law, natural law, or
common sense, to conceive of itself as an absolute, dominant
entity or despot which, whether the fault of an individual who
becomes a self-appointed dictator, a democratically elected
majority which acts like an abusive dictatorship, or a coalition
of various democratic parties that in fact act unilaterally, gives
the impression of an omnipotent being with only rights and no
duties. No, the state (together with its various legislative, executive, judicial, and other components) also has duties and
should be guided by healthy, ethical criteria that take the form
of service to the common good of its citizens, honesty, justice
and the respect of people's human rights.

A digression on the religious dimension of the state

I have said nothing about religious criteria as it might easily be
misconstrued and give the impression that I believed a model of
denominational state were needed. No, I do not believe this

because the teachings of the Second Vatican Council and the Popes on the subject are clear: the Church only requires freedom, not privilege. Furthermore, I should remind the reader that it is just as wrong for a non-denominational state to be anti-religious and persecute religious individuals and institutions, as it is for a denominational state to hinder or restrict the practice of other religions. Sadly enough, both do and have happened.

I put forward two points of view. Firstly, that if certain non-denominational states, instead of hindering the teaching of religion and spending immense sums of money on things that go against Christ's gospel, would foster good habits, and if certain government leaders demonstrated more virtue instead of lack of compassion for the poor, then their countries would run better and they would not need the mountains of money they employ in armies, police forces, jails, etc. There would be neither rich people who were too rich nor poor people who were too poor. Everyone would be more comfortable and safer in their homes and on the streets. Remember, the gospel is inexpensive. And also, why not admit it, with more gospel there would be less devastation caused by legalised abortions, terrorism, thieves of all kinds, etc. Secondly, if only all states, even non-denominational ones, would really respect and foster the human and civil right of the freedom of religious belief, they would indirectly be doing the best thing possible for the common good of society, without having to raise taxes. I can see that I am getting carried away and had better get back to the matter at hand.

What Rights and Duties Does a Nation Have?

I am speaking about nation and state in general, and have yet to finish. I ask myself, what rights and duties does a nation have? If we are dealing with a nation that has arisen and developed simultaneously as a single nation and a state, there is nothing more to add to what I have already said. I shall repeat it though, by way of summary: vis-à-vis the state itself, in the full enjoyment of its rights, it should respect those of its citizens, oblige them to fulfil their duties (social, financial, cultural, etc.) and, in all circumstances, seek the common good of society. As regards other states (whether neighbours or otherwise), its rights, among others, are: to be allowed to live in peace; to have its borders, if they are just, respected; to be free of financial persecution; to be protected by international treaties, etc. As far as duties are concerned, above all it must respect the legitimate rights of other nations.

The answers to the questions that may come up in the following pages could be more complicated. They are not for me and my convictions, but others with training and experiences different from my own may find them so.

The Plurinational State

Transition

I have said that a nation is such because it has characteristic features or details that make a specific human group become one in reality, and without which it could not come about, namely: its own language; a culture that, for centuries, has been distinct from other cultures; a unique history; and a series of further factors that show that its stature, as a social group, is truly different from the rest. To this, add the citizens' awareness of the reality and validity of these differences, the will to preserve them and their demand for respect by other groups, who in turn have their own characteristics, but different ones. If, in addition to this, the nation is independent of all other groups, we then have the figure of the state.

However, if it does not have full self-government, but is dependent on another nation which is an independent state, then the nation is not a state, yet it does not necessarily cease being a true nation. It only ceases to be a nation when its national values disappear because of lethargy, voluntary renunciation or the violent action of stronger states, for example, genocide, systemic and persistent deportations, the scientific application of genetic methods to lower birth rates that are subsequently made up for by a flood of citizens from other groups, etc.[2]

---

[2]This is different from what we could call 'evolving integration', the result of dignified dialogue and co-operation between equal nations who, true to their characteristic desire to open up and from a genuine grounding of identity, construct a subsequent macro-national group. Needless to say, this new grouping restructures their respect and respects the new structure. I am thinking here, for example, of a possible future Europe formed as a true family of peoples.

Concept

I cannot continue without also drawing attention to the concept of the plurinational state: a state that is not made up of one single nation, but of various nations. This is a possibility that does not imply any contradictions whatsoever and, in some cases, is not only possible but desirable and real. Its viability, as I say, does not involve absurd concepts, as perhaps many believe. However, it is true that a truly plurinational state is more complicated than a state made up of only one nation. If a state encompasses two territories, each inhabited by people who have features or values that make a human group, not just any group but a culturally differentiated community, a people, and if these characteristic features have not just appeared overnight as merely passing ideological or political phases, but are reasonable, valid, historical facts which the inhabitants living in each territory can perceive, observe and defend then, in these circumstances, it is a plurinational state. And if, within a state, instead of two territories with the characteristics described above there are more (it does not matter how many), this plurinationalism will be even more pronounced. I did mention that a plurinational state is obviously more prone to difficulties than a uninational state: history confirms as much, and reflection and study hold no surprises. However, these difficulties are not created by greater numbers, rather, they arise from the choices and errors of mankind and, always, in the end, from the lack or scarcity of true love amongst men.

Presentation

Imagine a state consisting of two nations: one, having all the natural, historical, cultural conditions for being one, not to mention various, more or less reasonable ethical, historical factors, which has achieved the status of sovereignty; and another also enjoying its own values, historical, cultural, etc., that are distinct from the former, but which, for various more or less debatable historical reasons, is currently not fully self-governing, even though at some point it may have enjoyed this condition of independent power, and lives within a state framework inherent to the first nation. What could one deduce or say of this situation? Let's deal with three real attitudes.

Three Types of Nationalism

In the first part I described three attitudes *before* a specific type of nationalism (aggressive), now I will move on to describe, with a certain amount of digression, three of the various species *of* nationalism which form the basis for my thoughts.

1. Intense Aggressive Nationalism

Description

Overview

The first attitude or type is represented by the nation that, as well as being one, has acquired the nature of a state in the course of its historical evolution and has the necessary organisation, power within its borders, acceptance and recognition by some of the other states, yet ignores that there is another nation – or various nations – within its territory that preserves its own characteristics. It not only ignores this but, furthermore, does not admit it. It does not allow the use of the name 'nation'. The state is divided into departments or provinces created around a ministry table with lines on a map. Perhaps it tolerates talk of regions. Natural, ancient, rooted differential factors such as language, culture, etc., are heavily persecuted, not admitted or ignored, depending on the mood of the government. Among others, the administrative idea of this first attitude or type contains the following components.

Specifics

a) Only one nation governs in the territory and is identified with the state. b) The state only contains provinces, which are decreed to be equal. c) Regions are admitted if they have no other value than being a mere sum or group of provinces. d) The state idolises unity. e) This unity of state only tolerates one manifestation: uniformity. Institutions should be equal or identical, depending on the case at hand, in accordance with the model the state has adopted, the model being based, of course, on the larger most powerful group or nation – the most typical example of this is usually language. f) Unity that is not uniform and pursued through the gradual absorption and disappearance of the differential factors of the nation or nations dominated by the state, is not allowed. Those, then, who seek unity of state, which the state needs to organise and defend itself, but reject uniformity, are to be considered dangerous citizens and subjected to special sanctions. g) Independent ideas and forms for the national territories lying within the state are persecuted. Political parties that advocate them are not permitted and clandestine movements favouring the creation of autonomous communities are rigorously harassed. h) The state defends the idea and fact of uniform unity: directly and using all the force and means in its power; indirectly over time and using efficient, tactical means that erode and discredit the distinctive personality of the non-state nations, especially language and culture. The objective is to bring about the loss of influence of the values of the nation or nations without statehood and replace them with the values of the nation-state.

Summary

Insofar as this attitude is concerned, customs and values that do not pertain to the nation-state are not considered riches, but a danger. The richness and diversity of cultural factors and values does not come into play. What matters is that the people of the nation that is not a state become accustomed to the characteristics of the nation-state and end up assimilating them. Achieving uniformity is considered a guarantee of unity, of power and riches by the state. Unity, according to this first attitude towards the relationship between the nation-state and the non-state nation or nations it contains, is achieved and maintained on the basis of eradicating the traditional values of the latter and laying down and maintaining an order subject to the absolute will of the dominant nation by laws and force. I could go further into this first attitude or type, but this is enough to go on. It is not an imaginary or invented description, these are real historical facts.

Unacceptability

From the perspective of the individual

What should we make of such a harsh attitude on the part of the nation-state towards non-state nations existing within its territory?

This first attitude is unacceptable, unjust and wrong. It is wrong in concept, and more so in its application. This attitude or type ignores, or marginalises, the true concept of the human being recognised, accepted and respected by modern-day, genuine democracies, and explained and proclaimed by the Magisterium of the Church, both by the Second Vatican Council and the Popes of our times.

The human being, wherever he lives on this Earth, enjoys a special dignity which men cannot give nor take away because it is conferred solely by God. The power of men, particularly the state, can neither grant nor take away the special dignity of the human being because it is permanent, from conception in the mother's womb till the time of death, but unjust power may fail to recognise this dignity and abuse it. It can do so, and has done so with great frequency. Human dignity comes from God, who bestows man with rights that are not given by the authorities, science or the skill of men. What men can do is fail to respect them and hinder the proper exercise of these rights, something which has and does take place. The individual is born not in a state but, primarily, in a nation. It is the nation that leaves its stamp first on the characteristics of the new-born child, not the state.

Allow me to add, in a similar vein and in parenthesis, that neither the state, nor doctors nor lawyers are ones to claim that, for example, on day 1 of week X a human being can be killed because, formally, he is not yet a man or an individual, and that on day 2 of week X he can no longer be killed ('the voluntary interruption of pregnancy', to me, seems a cynical euphemism), because he is now considered to be human. Very often the works of men contradict the works of God, but in the end it will be God who will be right and have the final word.

The infringement of common rights

The individual is born in his nation with rights conferred and respected by the Creator that, unfortunately, are very often not recognised by others who are sick in spirit and ride roughshod over the rights of the weakest driven by selfishness. If you are half-way observant of modern-day life, you will notice with horror how cases abound where someone infringes the human rights of another, making ridicule of any one of the ten commandments. Sadly, social institutions are also guilty of this, and never miss the chance to do so. While the highest institution, the state, whose very purpose is to serve its citizens and respect their rights, though it must be said it often tries and succeeds, will nevertheless also frequently violate these rights (it is always in the news), and, to cap it all, does so heavy handedly and with security and impunity. It is the same old story: lack of respect for the dignity of the individual, and a total lack of justice and love. The dignity of the human being and his rights will have difficulty making headway if his only recourse is to the letter of the Constitution and its laws. By exercising natural law, urged on by a clear conscience, and the law of love, taught by Jesus, human dignity would be in a better state.

The infringement of individual rights

Because of their dignity, human beings also enjoy other rights that are not common and equal, but arise in special circumstances such as, for example, belonging to a fatherland/motherland (the land of one's ancestors), a culture, a nation, etc. Important details that make them different, as individuals and as a group, from others living in different circumstances. A typical example is the natural language or idiom of the country of one's parents. People in the nation-state love their own, which is logical and how it should be, but likewise people in the non-state nation love theirs too.

The first type or attitude towards relations, between the nation-state and a non-state nation forming part of a single state, is not marked by its positive attitude to the rights in question. This attitude does not accept the plurality of nations in a state, does not believe it possible or reasonable and, in the manner it thinks best, persecutes it. In contrast, it assumes prerogatives that it has arbitrarily created to destroy the legitimate rights of the non-state nations, which because of their inferior position, they most likely lose. This unjust attitude may be considered normal in the state; perhaps because it is fearful of suspected dangers hovering over the uniformly-conceived unity of the state; it may even be the result of animosity or hate.

Resistance as a form of reaction

The fact

The lines above discuss the behaviour of the state, but not what the integrated 'non-state' nation or nations do or are able to do. The dominant state only accepts provinces that forgo their nationality and allow themselves to be assimilated and standardised for the nation state.

The birth of a plurinational state is an event that belongs to history, experienced by people in other times. These people may be admired or criticised, you may feel sorry for them, we can learn a few lessons from their experiences, but we cannot help them. In contrast, we as contemporaries are making history with our successes and failures, and we are in a position to help one another.

Its nature

The nation or nations that manage to preserve all or the majority of their traditional national characteristics and are subject to a plurinational state which thinks and acts as described in the first attitude or type mentioned, react or can react in a variety of ways, depending on the situation. The reader will have observed that the end result and means employed by the nation-state are harsh and all have the same goal: that the nations that are not state should disappear as nations, lose their characteristic values and become provinces, something which is impossible without violating human rights. It is therefore normal for them to react, if they are fully aware of their situation, by defending themselves, as all living beings defend themselves from attack.

The ethics: the need for honest means

The natural, rational right of self-defence by non-state nations subject to a stronger nation-state also presupposes the duty to exercise this right using reasonable means, as long as they do not fall into the trap or make the mistake of defending themselves from rights abuses on the part of an aggressive state by abusing the latter's own rights as the nation attacked. If it is not right to attack by transgressing another's rights, then it is also not right to respond by unduly inflating one's own rights. A dishonest act is not morally rectified by dishonest acts. It is good not evil that can and should remedy human misery. It is very difficult for violence, in more or less visible and dramatic varieties (some highly refined), not to engender further violence or an even worse situation than the one it was supposed to prevent or improve upon.

The question of a just war is not an easy one to answer, and I do not consider it appropriate to discuss here. The pros and cons, which in any case tend to be better understood once a war is over, would need to be very carefully sized up and analysed. Cries like 'better to die on your feet than live on your knees' and other similar slogans, seem to me, feeble in content; I very much like my life, despite its being sometimes so hard, and I very much love and value the lives of others, even if they are enemies – so teaches Christ. There are many alternatives to war and battle, some perhaps unknown because they have not been searched for or required by God's will. Even in a nation that, for whatever reason, is not a sovereign state and has undergone much frequent, harsh struggle and suffering, it is still possible for an individual to lead a normal life, to behave as an honourable, holy person and to love and do good for others, and many have pressed on in this way. Of course, this refers to a state that, despite its oppressive status, has not reached the extremes of genocide. Under this kind of state one barely survives.[3]

---

[3]In *Populorum Progressio*, 31 (1967) Paul VI wrote the following, 'Nevertheless, as is well known, revolutionary insurgency – except in cases of evident, prolonged tyranny that seriously assaults the fundamental rights of the individual and dangerously damages the common good of a country – engenders new injustices, introduces new imbalances and provokes further ruin. A real wrong cannot be fought at the price of a greater wrong.' The basic assertion of this quote is found outside the parenthesis. It is the thesis I defend in this book. Nevertheless, the parenthesis has an element of truth. The Magisterium does not forget the right of self-defence, the recourse to force, the innocent unjustly attacked, whether an individual or a group. However, this requires very strict conditions, which are listed here: a) evident, prolonged tyranny; b) a serious assault on the fundamental rights of the individual; and c) dangerous harm to the common good. I believe that these conditions are not found in the current context of the Spanish state.

Relinquishment

The loss of national conscience

What can be said about the case of a nation that, integrated into a powerful state skilled in the business of assimilation, has lost and forgotten its awareness and will as a nationality? There was perhaps a time, many years previously, when the people had enjoyed a clear idea of being a nation, but the strategy of the dominant nation totally or partially sapped the traditional values of the dominated nation or nations. The language was discredited and persecuted by the dominant language. It was thought fit for the home but rid from the fair fields of culture. It was accused of being inappropriate for learned, distinguished and aristocratic people. It was eliminated from the schools, from centres of learning, from official bodies, and it was even possible to eradicate it from the religious sphere (catechism, preaching and worship, etc.). Over the years, after a string of similar, excessive occurrences, some or many of the citizens were affected by loss of memory, an inferiority complex, the imposition of 'new trends' and a lack of interest in 'the past'.

The state is powerful in its means and ways to destroy all that is a hindrance to the nation that sees itself as the backbone of the state and only significant figure. If things come to this sad pass, there is the likelihood that the people in the subordinated nation will lose interest in their traditional national characteristics, stop caring about them and give in to the current social, cultural, religious, working, business, leisure and entertainment trends set by the population in the nation-state. The nations I refer to may as well die out, or just devote themselves to preserving superficial folklore memories that pose no threat to state power, the jealous custodian of a unity that it interprets as sameness and uniformity.

The causes of passive assimilation

In a process of decline of national values and thriving racism within a plurinational state there is nearly always, or at least frequently, an even more major factor, which can lead to scenarios of disapproving coexistence. This is not mere uninterestedness but something far worse: disdain for the values of their own nation and an eagerness to assimilate the points of view, opinions and characteristics of the nation-state. Those who adopt this attitude feel comfortable in the new scenario, so unlike that of their ancestors. They believe they are good and true to themselves – in the right. And whenever something comes up that is awkward or otherwise, they support not their own nation, but the side of the nation-state.

There are a variety of reasons why these people may feel good or better about the characteristics of the nation-state in whose territory they live side by side. For example: lack of knowledge about the history of the nation to which they belong as their ancestors' descendants; an uncritical knowledge of the history of the nation-state that they have come to adopt (I say 'uncritical' because the historians of over-bearing nation-states tend to be economical with the truth and dress up the facts: instead of serving humble but annoying truth, they glorify with enthusiastic patriotism that is sure to please); another reason may be family inheritances received in exchange for political favours or who knows what; also, over time, fearfulness of the insignificance of one's nation and a desire for grandeur, will help contribute to the mutation; or the fear of being filed on police records, of persecution, of discrimination, etc. Whatever the causes of the change, the reality is that those who belonged to a nation because of lineage or specific values, have now renounced it and opted for the values of the other nation. These new values may be good and noble, and it may be reasonable to expect that a citizen should love them, but they are seriously devalued if the rights of another nation or nations forming part of the nation-state are scorned and persecuted. It is evident – though others may dispute it – that no nation has the right to take possession of another nation's territory, or either totally or partially destroy traditional values that have been honourably kept without harm to anyone.

A wrong dangerous stance

What can be said about those citizens who have lost touch with their national roots? My purpose is not to judge people, whom I respect and love, and much less would I wish to take a jab at their conscience or duty, their deeper and most inner thoughts only God can know. But I would like to express my opinion on the influence or deeds of people and citizens. Might I add that I have no difficulty in recognising that I may be mistaken.

I believe, therefore, that the position of these citizens is wrong and dangerous. Wrong because these people, who I assume are acting in goodwill and in an upright manner, are accomplices to unjust behaviour, to the infringement of human rights committed by the aggressor nation-state on the subject nation or nations. They reinforce and keep alive the view or conviction that the way the dominant nation-state conducts its affairs is for the common good and does not quash any presumed rights of the nations it embraces. Dangerous because, in addition to other drawbacks, it may spark trouble, hatred and extreme behaviour among the citizens of the subject nation; specifically, between the defenders of their rights and the supporters of a state that does not recognise them.

Summary of attitudes

As you can see, I am not writing to accuse or attack. I solely ask and recommend people not to view the subject of nationalist philosophies in a plurinational state from a particular fixed standpoint, but to go over the arguments in question thoroughly: study the histories of the nations in the plurinational state; ensure you have a good understanding of the dignity of the human being and all his true rights; clarify both the concepts of the common good and the rights of the state as their defender and champion; and insist on the exercise of true democracy, because some forms of democracy, with suspect governing majority parties and coalitions, contain heavy undertones of dictatorship.

If the citizens are believers, they should study these issues in the light the Catholic Magistracy. They will see how objectively and clearly these concepts can be applied and will, perhaps, notice that their opinions (whether as government leaders or citizens) are not as sure and solid as they believed. Let them undertake this examination, not to the advantage or disadvantage of one side or the other, but so that conflict and hatred may disappear and respect, tolerance, justice, peace and love may spread.

I would feel my efforts have been fully rewarded if there were just one citizen who, by becoming aware of his dislike, hatred or even nationalist xenophobia, had the goodness of heart and courage to renounce these feelings and spend some time calmly and thoroughly examining the reasons for his attitudes.

The disease of aggressive nationalist philosophies can only be cured by a desire for truth, large doses of respect, a deep sense of justice, intense Christian love – including love of one's enemies – and, as a result of all this, true peace.

Conclusion

This concludes my reflections on the first type or attitude and the relationships between nations coexisting in a plurinational state. It is the harshest and least reasonable attitude. It shows a clear, important and very real difference between two types of nationalism: a country or nation that defends its traditional values without infringing the values of another nation, using violent means or the abuse of power to do so – defensive nationalism; and aggressive nationalism that not only loves and defends the values that characterise the nation itself, which is worthy and just, and a legitimate right, but that also arrogates for itself the erroneous right to disregard the traditional values of other nations and fight them with violent tactics and means in order to destroy them or reduce them to insignificance.

The most curious thing about this division is that usually only the individuals and nationalist parties that defend themselves tend to be called 'nationalists' by the dominant group – a word they consider pejorative or dangerous – when, in reality, it is those individuals and plurinational state parties and governments who not only assert themselves but also attack others who should also be the ones, especially, to call themselves 'nationalists' – an exacerbated form, to be sure, because they practise an unjust form of nationalism. When is nationalism pejorative? When it defends its values? Or when it attacks another's values?

2. Attenuated Aggressive Nationalism

Description

With this second type, the principles and ideas of the nation-state are generally the same as in the first, but they are not held and applied with such harshness. So long as there is nothing happening to raise tempers, people's lives go on in relative normality and we see no disruption to their ordinary activities, working lives, everyday problems and pleasures. Ideas and feelings on state and nation persist, but only as smouldering embers covered, to a greater or lesser extent, by the ashes of other more pressing concerns.

In this second type, dictatorships have been done away with and democracy has been adopted. Democracy can affect parliament, government, parties, the media, the Constitution and laws in different ways. The situation can, on the one hand, lead to calm because there are none of the awful conditions found under dictatorships, and on the other hand give an impression of uproar whenever the political parties and the media, who are not quite in agreement or who openly disagree on nationalism, launch themselves into argument beyond a reasonable limit.

Observations

Anyway, the situation with this type is very clear: there is a very real state nationalism – despite the fact that government leaders, Constitution or citizens in total compliance with this type refuse to acknowledge the label – which ignores or explicitly rejects the existence of a nation or nations within its borders, considering them solely as territorial or provincial communities with equal rights and responsibilities. There is also a further type of nationalism – which state nationalism does not recognise and which it persecutes in a fairly veiled manner – that lacks its own state or self-government and whose traditional national values must be defended within the limits set by democracy. The latter are not protected by the nation-state as values and rights in themselves but, quite the contrary, to a greater or lesser degree as times and trends dictate.

With this type of nation and nationalism, the characteristic values of the nation-state enjoy all the advantages state power offers and are financed from the pockets of all who belong to the cultures and languages existing within it. The latter must fend for their own survival and it is of little help that the democratic structure permits it. The result of this precarious situation often leads to exactly what the nation-state wants to see: traditional national values other than its own are not rated by the state, and other's values are no longer appreciated, lie dormant or die out.

If a significant portion of its citizens in the dominated nations preserve their memories well, have the drive and resources, then their nationalism may survive for years and centuries and may even, at some future date, be reawakened, fostered by changes and special circumstances. If this situation does not present itself, and government is sufficiently skilful and destructive, the nations and nationalisms may disappear, just as, on the other hand and in a different sense, states can change frontiers and forms because nothing is eternal in human reality.

3. Recognition and Respect in Plurinationalism

The state adopts the right attitude

I would like to conclude this section with a few notes on a third attitude or type of nationalism within a plurinational state. Here, the state neither wishes to ignore, nor does ignore or persecute the nation or nations with their own traditional values – which can be summed up in the term 'differential factor'. It does not ignore or reject them: it acknowledges, recognises and respects them instead as a social fact and on an official basis, as part of a constitutional prescription. The reason for this step or change would be tedious to explain or comment upon, but it is easy to see as a reality: nations or nationalities exist, are recognised and encouraged and are capable of dialogue and co-operation with the willing consent of the state.

The dominant nation recognises and respects sister nations

The larger, dominant nation, in full possession of its rights, advances by loving itself and its nationalism, but also recognises and is clearly conscious that it is a nation and not a super-nation that, better off through circumstance, is unique or master of the others. It realises that the state does not exist solely to grant its nation all the benefits and deny them to the others. The nation-state, guardian and driving force of the general welfare, must consider the prosperity of all the nations it embraces, as sisters who love, know and help one another, and who have forged a common history or shared inheritance – as sisters, not lady of the house and maid. It should look on the variety of cultural characteristics as a true wealth held in common. It should not persecute these varied manifestations of culture as a hindrance, but foster them as values. It should reject the highly fallacious argument that unity requires sameness (the latter impoverishes he who forcibly imposes it and harms he who endures it). This is because it is not natural for people who enjoy the wealth of language and culture granted by Providence to be deprived of values that are their own, thereby enriching the size, and only the size, of those who are already quite rich enough in values granted by the self-same Providence, nature and history.

It is right and fitting that the state should seek, foster and protect unity, so that peace can reign and thus benefit progress, but, evidently, union and peace between citizens can and should be sought through procedures that do not discriminate or create enmity and suffering. Treating all nations as good and equal is the best way to achieve union and unity.

The governors of the state, the other nations, the differential factor

The government leaders of a plurinational state should avoid any bias to the benefit of the powerful nation and the detriment of another's sensibilities, otherwise there will certainly be unrest. Animosity and hatred should likewise be prevented and, if they have already existed for a while, they should be seriously examined and the best possible steps taken to temper and rid society of them, as they can lead to much harm. The recent examples we have witnessed of the former Yugoslavia on a nationalist stage and Rwanda on its tribal/national stage, give an idea of the dangers posed by large masses inflamed by hatred, intensified in modern times by such powerful media and those who control and manipulate it.

The least favoured nation or nations defending their national rights and vitality eventually come up against problematic situations. They should be aware that life follows a natural course of rights and duties giving preference to the common good above personal welfare and advantage. The understanding and respect needed to live together in a recognised democratic plurinationality is easier to prescribe than to take as a medicine. The secret lies in love. If the individual is capable of truly loving, he will understand and respect. If we do not begin with this valuable component, cohabitation can become very bitter.

These few ideas on the relationships between nations living within the territory of the plurinational state, presupposing a democratic state that recognises, *de facto* and *de jure*, the so-called differential factor, refer to the facet that interests me, namely: the ethical dimension, the reality of these factors and the required behaviour that these factors imply or demand. In short: a good understanding of the factors, rights and duties, and following these precepts as best one can. This does not involve conflict, attacks, ignorance, abuse of the media, lies, insults, deep hatred or any other such similar behaviour.

A climate of dialogue and love

The only way of dealing with serious, thorny issues between people, and the only honourable, honest and elegant way of tackling and solving them, is through dialogue that meets all the conditions. Among these, I would like to remind the reader of the ones, duly adapted, laid down by the Magisterium of the Catholic Church, in a pontifical document that made history, *Ecclesiam suam* (1964), which taught: clarity, serenity, trust and prudence. In addition, one needs to take into account one's own limitations and be humble enough to suspect that perhaps the other party is more intelligent or at least not as ignorant or bad as he is made out to be.

There are others, but the decisive condition is that there should be no lack of love. Love in the clean, evangelical sense of the word, because, as we all know, the world is full of ambiguous, foolish loves and, harsh though it might be to say so, the work of some or many Christians and what they think is Christian love is manifestly fairly distant or far from it.

In any case, for there to be love and no hot or cold wars in a plurinational state, three main conditions – in addition to other less basic ones – are absolutely necessary. Firstly: understanding and, therefore, truly recognising the fact of plurinationality. History, whether ancient or contemporary should not be unknown, inaccurately reported or distorted; those who can and should stamp out ignorance have a duty and responsibility to do so. Secondly: there is to be no fighting, lies, arousal of hatred, organising campaigns or recurring to repulsive, mediocre means that excite the masses and political parties, as these are always harmful to truth and peace. Third condition:

the presence of much love. You cannot stray from these duties. Is this not supreme valour? What does Christ say about the love He teaches? Where is love to be seen in certain writers, certain media, certain cries to patriotism, in people who speak as if they monopolised the truth? I am aware that to many these ideas may sound naive, utopian, trite, or a way to make accusation. But anyone who is scornful of these conditions will not succeed in resolving problems of this nature.

The question of structures

How should a plurinational state structure itself in the best possible way – democratically and politically – for the good of all groups? I do not believe that the most fitting person to answer this question is someone who proposes only to remember that there are human groups whom we call nations; that there are forms of nationalism that, in all justice, are correct and others that are not – what the Church Magistracy terms 'exacerbated'; that the former have the right to exist and that the latter should be avoided by examining, learning, reviewing and bringing up to date, for ethical, religious or whatever motives. Similarly to be avoided are those moods that create animosity, hatred, enmity, xenophobia – forestalling or curing them by applying good, efficient therapy. These are points that make sense to me or I am beholden to as a Christian contemplating earthly realities through the eyes of the Gospel.

The answer, therefore, to the above question on how to currently structure or how to evolve towards better structures in national bodies, should be given by citizens from all groups – not just those in the more powerful group by virtue of their power and strength. It should be given by political parties in the programmes they present, by experts from the various branches of human knowledge – lawyers, politicians, economists, etc. Priests, bishops and religious people, as such, are not builders of lay structures; they can and should be prophetic voices to be listened to when lay institutions misuse their authority, riding roughshod over human rights actively or by ignoring them.

The Subject of Independence

General Criteria

Can a nation without state aspire to independence?

Can a nationality that forms part of and is accepted by a state evolve with time and circumstances towards independence, showing that there are necessary and sufficient reasons to have it?

In all sincerity and freedom I would answer: firstly, that my objective is not to stir up problems or start disputes, but to prevent very distressing and lamentable wrongs that come from, at least in part, a lack of clear concepts which the citizenry needs to understand and live by.

However, this said, secondly I would add that the concept or word independence does not tend to get good press, especially in a non-homogenous state made up of more than one group with national characteristics, or 'differential factors'. It is over-whelmingly looked upon as wrong, bad, an offence, treason; an aspiration to be combated as the worst of all possible evils. According to this opinion, unity is sacred, frontiers are invio-lable, state weapons and forces need to be ready and willing to annihilate any outbreak of disintegration in the state using violence, etc.

Very well then, and this is my third answer, I believe that those who think like this, or express similar ideas, are making a number of errors, have no conception of the complexities involved and do not have their ideas clear. Why?

We need to distinguish

The concept of 'independence' is not always a 'holy' notion, nor always an 'evil' one. It is an 'ambiguous' concept, that depends on circumstance. For example: when Russian Tsars or Soviet communists seized independent nations and subjugated them for many years through wars, wasn't it natural for those nations to seek independence? Was its movement of independence evil? When the Reich, first, and Nazi Germany, later, seized Poland, did the Poles not have the right to claim independence?

Is independence wrong? We could go over the history of the two terrible world wars and see how the victors created states and nations according to their interests, setting frontiers on maps. 'Holy' frontiers? Take care, then, when blessing or damning a concept seen only through one-colour glasses.

There can be independence movements that are good in some circumstances and bad in other circumstances. There is no independence movement that is 'good because it is' or 'bad because it is'. They need to be judged by the circumstances at hand, not by emotion and prejudice. Having said this, I wish to make it perfectly clear that it is an overreaction to then disparage or blame a person or group for believing in independence or accuse them of seeking independence. Complicated realities should not be dealt with by using knee-jerk reactions, superficial judgements or exaggerated qualifying terms. It is true, I believe and reiterate, that when dealing with independence, nationalism and autonomies, we cannot act from a standpoint of (very commonly) ignorance, or (also very commonly) passion, nor with prejudiced ideas thought to be fixed but are not. We need instead to act with understanding and a genuine sense of criticism, calmly and peacefully, with respect and love for God and one's fellow man.

My Personal Position

I am a Spaniard

I suspect that some of my Spanish-speaking brothers – who possess a language of great stature that forms a constituent part of their nation, though is not the only one – will be scandalised on reading my words, as, for them, this is all very new and disagreeable, and will think that the person saying these things is an enemy of Spain, a detestable separatist. Well, no, it would be mistake to adopt such an attitude. I am no enemy of Spain. I am a Spaniard who perhaps loves Spain more than others who would solve everything with the cry 'Long live Spain!' and, when called upon to prove their patriotic fervour with honest, dignified and fair action, forget their love and stubbornly stick to their dislike of Catalans.

I am a Spaniard and I respect and admire the national values of language and culture in the Castilian nation. I love its language, which was not created by the Spanish state but born with the Castilian people out of a variety of circumstances centuries ago, before the state existed, just like other languages such as, for example, the Catalan tongue, which is not a dialect, as we were taught at school, but a rich language with an abundant literature that goes all the way back to its beginnings.

I love all the values and traditions of the other nationalities and regions in the state, and I have a high regard for many Castilian people whose friend I am honoured to be, who are also fond of me and with whom I have never had any problems over the subject of different national values. During many years of episcopal ministry I have attempted to love and serve people from all regions and nationalities who were in difficulties, who have adapted very well, who have respected my language and culture, and who have acted with more gratitude than my help could deserve. I ask you to pardon me for what may come over as a lack of personal modesty. It is not – in fact it was a pleasure simply to fulfil my duty: not to discriminate against my brothers, but above all to love them as I do myself.

A personal detail

Given the simple, epistolary style that I am using in these notes, I would like to recollect something very personal that may reinforce my declaration of respect and esteem for all things Castilian in Spain. It is a small devout revelation that few know of. Since 21 March 1931 – youth, that divine treasure! – I have always worn a simple metal crucifix with an inscription in Latin on the back, almost illegible with the years, saying, '*Sac. e. P. Coll. HIsp. 21 Martii 1931*' (Priest of the Spanish Pontifical College, 21 March 1931). Indeed, I was ordained presbyter in the Basilica of Saint John Lateran, Rome, on this date. I have never taken off the crucifix, either in the day or at night, not even during the terrible religious persecution of 1936, when I knew that I was condemned to die. I also knew that, if found in my hiding hole, I would have been killed whether I wore the crucifix or not, just as they killed another sick, old priest who was in the same house.

This crucifix, along with its many memories, was given to me by the priest and rector of the Spanish College in Rome, Don Pedro Ruiz de los Paños, a worthy man of many good qualities, who we as seminarists very much appreciated because we knew that behind his seriousness he hid how much he loved us. At the end of the war, I learnt that persecution had caught up with him in Spain and that he had been murdered for the same crimes that they had wanted to murder me for. I entrust myself to his prayers. Very well then, Don Pedro, a true Castilian, was a man who respected and loved everyone. And this is what matters. I loved him and I continue to love him, in the communion of saints.

Is the person writing this a separatist?

So should a reader of these pages ask the question, 'Is the person writing this someone seeking Catalan independence, a separatist?', I will first answer that I am neither surprised by nor upset by the question. I am well aware of how fond many people may be of identifying or confusing the terms Catalan and separatist. I have just been reminded of it. It does not surprise or upset me, but it saddens me because it shows how deep down the ignorance and, sometimes, the anti-Catalan phobia lies within people.

Added to which, I will repeat: I am not a separatist, I never have been, and, in the remaining short time allotted me, I do not believe I am likely to change my mind. However, this does not stop me from thinking out loud in this manner. Perhaps, once we are well into the twenty-first century, my position might be different, because, really, the term 'independence supporter' does not horrify me or make me shiver as it does others, nor do I consider it an 'evil concept' or sinful. Independence at the human level is a natural and just thing, especially when being independent means defending oneself from something or someone who, for whatever reason, is treating one unjustly. Furthermore, the growing evolution of peoples towards mutual interdependence helps put in perspective the current concept of the sovereignty of states. Very likely the Europe of the next century will be made up of an interactive framework where the current concept of independence will have lost its basic connotations in favour of a macro-community in which, without losing their personality, people will rediscover their motivation and their structures of interrelationship will be enhanced.

As for Spain, in particular, I believe that total political independence for Catalonia is not advisable in the light of social interrelationship and the history we hold in common. Not because Catalonia's dependency is in fact eternal, immutable or sacrosanct, as is sometimes claimed. Whoever said this today would, I believe, assert the same about Portugal, were it not for the Battle of Aljubarrota, an event that spelled change. Portugal has been independent for a long time, and when the Portuguese Head of State visits Madrid, he receives due honours.

It is not that I have ever hoped or wished for a victorious battle for Catalonia, or violence of any kind. I simply cite it as an example of how an event can change the political plans of men, which prove not to be as long-lasting and solid as the ethnic or national reality of peoples. I also mention it because violent victories and wars are not desirable, either for Catalonia (which I very much doubt any Catalan would wish), or for any other nationality or region in Spain. With goodwill and a good understanding of the situation, without hatred or obsessions, and healthy dialogue and democracy, many problems can – and should – be solved.

What would occur if the option for independence presented itself?

In a pluralistic, exemplary, democratic Spain, free of dogmatic declarations on nationalism, enjoying human rights, frontiers and federalism, a country populated by civilised, freedom-loving citizens who respected one another and showed no signs of being anti-something or anti-someone, free of phobias and the like, what would occur – unlikely and utopian hypothesis that it is – if Catalonia peacefully decided by absolute majority, unhindered by international organisations, on self-determination or independence after holding free elections or referenda?

I am not in a position to reply to this hypothetical question, as unlikely as these circumstances would be in our times. I doubt that many other people are in a position to do so either, although there would be plenty of irate or laughable answers. I pose the question only to show that, in the past and the future, there are no political truths you can take as faithfully revealed dogma and so we need to be more conscious of factors such as wisdom, circumstance and, in particular, the fact that Providence has a decisive hand in everything.

However, in every hypothesis, whether of Spanish plurina-tionality – my own – or of independence, what indeed is a perennial moral truth is that the peoples in question should open up to one another, love each other as brothers, co-operate efficiently and together seek a higher common good that enriches and is an inevitable requirement.[4] Where this has always been true, it is even more so in today's double climate of a European Union under construction and a planet whose growing unity is more and more essential and, too, the increasing need for respect and furtherance of all its peoples and cultures.

He who understands this point will grasp the yearning for decisive unity – in truth, justice, love, freedom and equality for all nations – that fills these pages.[5]

---

[4]The already quoted document *Arrels cristianes de Catalunya* (The Christian Roots of Catalonia) states, 'It should be said that, in remembering the need to clarify between the concepts of the nation and the state for the sake of an accurate interpretation of present-day realities, we do not intend to reduce the ties of brotherhood and solidarity between the peoples of Spain to a purely administrative relationship. Our common history, with all that is good in it and all that has been negative, our interrelationships, swelled in our times by migration, our major underlying affinities, in which our shared faith plays an extremely important role, have all woven a solid basis for understanding, affection and co-operation between us all. However, it will only be possible to move forward if the political and administrative forms adopted by the state do not at any time hinder the natural development of each people but, instead, benefit and serve them.' (p. 12)

[5]Basically, what is at stake, is that every true nation has the right to possess a state structure that fills it needs. This structure may be either uni-national or pluri-national. The greater or lesser convenience of one or the other depends as much on the importance of the subject as it does on circumstances, among them, clearly, historical factors. It, therefore, becomes a problem of justice and prudence. In any case, the final result has to be an interdependence between equals based on a superior common good, as I have noted above. In the light of this, a plurinational State can, certainly, 'fragment', 'decay' and 'break up', but it can also, by the calm, peaceful agreement of its component members, divide into two or more nations with their own state structures that coexist in harmony with one another. The exemplary separation of the Czech Republic and Slovakia demonstrate the historical viability of these assertions.

CHAPTER FOUR

THE FINAL QUESTION: WHAT ABOUT SPAIN?

First Overview: Presentation and Overall Reply

There are Several Nationalist Philosophies in Spain

Nations and states

I now come to my final question, what about Spain? Methodologically I have already advanced an answer and now I would like to go into more detail. There are several nationalist philosophies in Spain: they have existed for many years and I feel that, sick or healthy, they will continue to exist for a long time, if my concepts and vocabulary are found to be right. There are several nationalist philosophies in Spain because the state is made up of more than one nation. In each one of these the people, a majority, or a significant part of them, know, love, preserve and defend their valued characteristics, which are different from other similar human groups. This is very normal and praiseworthy.

What we call the characteristics of nationality or a nation are not goods created by the men and women who make up today's world, but ones inherited from their parents, and they from their parents in turn, and so on, all the way back through time, at no point being able to find the original group responsible for deciding and creating these values. By this I mean to say that these natural rights are not the simple fruit of an agreement, a royal wedding, a state, a purchase or prearranged deal such as, for example, by a state, government or policy. The traditional values of a nation arise prior to these types of decisions or actions and by their nature vary, change and easily perish. Nor are they eternal, but they take longer to expire than other human realities. The men, therefore, who have inherited these values, preserve them and have a strong desire to hold mastery over and take advantage of them, are proud of having them and are not prepared to let another national group destroy, persecute, mistreat or otherwise try to dispose of them.

When is nationalism within its just constraints?

If nationalism remains within its just constraints and means, surely this is not a bad thing and is therefore good? It is easy to see and say, though, unfortunately, not many may see it this way or be concerned enough to think about the question, and so deny it, leading in turn to thousands of other problems. Nationalism is within its just constraints and good when it not only loves and preserves its national values, but also respects the characteristic rights of other groups or nations owning similar values; long-lasting natural values that were not created by a state, and which it should not attack, persecute or destroy. Neither God, nor nature, nor the international community of states has granted any nation state the right to attack, persecute, hate or try to destroy another nation with true national values. These values only disappear or can disappear when the nation freely relinquishes them or when it is completely destroyed, assimilated or standardised by another more powerful nation that is a state.

In Spain there are groups that own, preserve and love their national values

In Spain, as in other countries, there are groups of people that own, preserve, love and defend different national values. They are therefore true nations or nationalities and each one has its own form of nationalism, which is not necessarily a bad thing – though it may have been given a bad reputation, through no fault of its own – so long as it stays within its just constraints and uses the right means of self-affirmation.

My Spanish-speaking readers will have noticed that in these pages I have attempted to state clearly that Spain has, and has had, various forms of nationalism, because it contains, at least, two nations and nationalities, one in Spanish-speaking territories. This nationality really exists, though perhaps neither the fact, the idea or the word is acknowledged. It forms the backbone of a nationalism that owns and defends its own rights (historical, present and acknowledged by the international community), that have not been challenged or persecuted by anyone (the Napoleonic invasion is not relevant here). This nation is a state, as many other nations in Europe also are. I should remind the reader again that a state is not the same thing as a nation, either in its forms and origins, or in its essential values.

Nations have created themselves in, you could say, almost mysterious complex ways over long periods of time and do not disappear or break up easily. Lying within them there is something long-lasting, natural, not created *a priori*, something that does not suddenly and deliberately rust away or die, or gladly tolerates its own disappearance or death through the violence of others. States, on the other hand, are power structures that are composed of a very high degree of conscious social organisation and a marked amount of mutability. States are formed over one or several nations on the basis of a variety of factors, wars, treaties, royal marriages, etc.

These ideas tend to be accepted by nations but not by certain states, reluctant to face the consequences of plurinationality. Say what you like, admit it or not, Spain, the part consisting of the old Crown of Castile which also forms the state and predominantly takes on the cultural characteristics of one, has on more than one occasion dealt very differently with the other nationalities, whose distinct features it has failed to take up with equal criteria when the natural, logical thing would have been not to limit or persecute them, but to respect and champion them.

The Castilian Nation and Radical Spanish Nationalism are not the Same Thing

Aggressive Spanish nationalism

I have given testament to my love of Castilian values and the people who quite rightly live them and love them. But now I need to add that the Castilian nation and the radical Castilian-Spanish nationalism identified with the state are not the same thing. We are dealing with a specific, strong, harsh nationalism, not only in terms of defending nature-given national rights, but also for attacking the rights and values of other nationalities, in our case, Catalan nationalism. This type of Spanish nationalism, which maintains an aggressive, destructive tradition towards the Catalan language and culture and all the other valued characteristics of the Catalan nation, is not good.[1]

Catalan Nationalism

A working hypothesis

Catalan nationalism defends its values and rights which it did not receive from the Spanish state, the Spanish language or Spanish culture. Catalan nationalism has not persecuted the language of

---

[1]Among others, the following texts constitute examples of this tradition (the italics are mine):

a) 'May Your Majesty take as the most important matter of His Monarchy the business of becoming King of Spain. By this I mean, Sir, that Your Majesty should not be content with being King of Portugal, of Aragón, of Valencia and Count of Barcelona, but should procure and consider with mute, secret council *to reduce these Kingdoms that make up Spain, to the manner and laws of Castile without difference.* Should Your Majesty achieve this He shall be the most powerful prince in the world.' (Secret memo by Count-Duke of Olivares to Felipe IV, 25 December 1624).

b) In instructions to the Chief Magistrates of Majorca and Catalonia (1717), King Felipe V requests that '... to skilfully attempt to introduce the Spanish language in those lands ... The Chief Magistrate shall take the greatest care to introduce the Spanish language, to which end *he shall bring to bear the most well-tempered and covert measures to achieve this end, so that the effect is achieved without drawing attention to the effort being exerted.*'

c) Carlos III, by Royal Decree of 23 June 1768, decided to collect 'the duty on procedural laws in Vellón reals throughout the Crown of Aragón, *and*

Cervantes, nor any part of Spanish culture. Catalan nationalism loves and defends its own and respects what belongs to others. It has never interfered in any other nationalism, imposing its language or inflicting its culture. An idea crops up in my mind, perhaps a naive one to my Spanish-speaking readers, but one that may help put things in perspective – a comparison which will not seem so simple-minded to my Catalan readers. Imagine if at some specific moment in its history, a vigorous, powerful Catalonia that was respected throughout the Mediterranean had walked the easy path of hegemony over other lands in the peninsula and, driven by the lust for dominion, had: forced the Spanish-speaking inhabitants to restrict the use of their language to the intimacy of their families; ordered schools and universities to only teach in Catalan; persecuted to death the public use of Spanish for long periods of time; reinforced the predominance of Catalan rights in all its conflicts; and, to cap it all, had tolerated an ingrained animosity towards Spanish values in its areas of influence that was passed down from generation to generation up to the present day. What would Castilian nationalists believe and say now (and they would be fully justified), after being exposed to similar conditions? You can imagine.

The Weeds of Old have been Sprouting Anew

Some facts

The sad thing is, that along with the revelry of these last few months, when least expected, the weeds of old have been

---

that all the Kingdom shall speak and learn the Spanish language'. On 22 September 1780, another decree declared 'that all the schools in the Kingdom shall teach children their native language, *as given by the grammar composed and published by the Royal Academy of Language'.* As we can see, the *native* language of all Spaniards had to be Castilian Spanish.

d) During the last century, the dictatorships of General Primo de Rivera and Franco blatantly perpetuated this overbearing tradition that is so characteristic of aggressive nationalism.

e) Fortunately, the Constitution of 1978 means a change of direction towards, not only a position of respect, but also one that promotes culture and language, as I set out in some detail further ahead.

N.B.: See Appendix Two: Political documents, texts a), b) and c) with slight variants, due to the different sources from which they come.

sprouting anew.[2] The media has seen an avalanche of rude comments, insults and jokes in very bad taste that have copiously poured from the mouths and pens of certain citizens who are not prepared to change the habits of their secular nationalism, individuals who are well-versed in the art of persecuting the Catalan values cherished and loved by its people, despite knowing, or they should know, that the majority of newspapers and books published in and exported from Barcelona are edited in the Spanish tongue. I do not want to get involved in the issue, and I have no wish to present a list of the many injustices and outrages suffered by Catalonia over its history – there are plenty of well-documented books to recall them. One only wishes that these extreme nationalists would read them: perhaps then they would understand why Catalonia defends itself and has no taste for attacking other cultures. I give only relative importance to the circumstances of everyday life and, for me, the sad events in old and modern-day history are not as significant as the attitudes they embody.

The anti-Catalan syndrome persists

In reality, what saddens me the most is what these events signify: the persistence of the 'anti-Catalan syndrome'. An inexplicable, disagreeable animosity which, judging by the force and sort of taunts and terms used, combines disdain and hatred. These attitudes cause great unhappiness because it is not pleasant for a Catalan throughout his life to feel that he is someone to be wary of or a public enemy – not just by one but many people, most of them probably good Christians who perhaps have no inkling of why they keep up such animosity. For a while, it seemed as if the historical climate of prejudice towards everything Catalan had improved, pressured by modern currents of feeling, which has spanned from the declaration of human rights by the UN to the documents produced by the Second Vatican Council, and the step forward taken by the State of the Autonomies, etc. However, events show this is not so in reality, and, as far as I know, these outrages have not warranted the effective disapproval or censure by many individuals and institutions that could and should have disavowed them.

---

[2]In 1994 some newspapers published in Madrid launched a campaign against Catalan nationalism and those seen to support it.

Worrying questions

Why does this unjust, malevolent tradition have to last so many years and centuries? What kind of original sin must Catalonia have committed at the dawn of history? Have the human rights of the Castilian nationality and associated groups, at any time, been ill-treated or persecuted by the forces of Catalan national-ity? Is it not obvious, in contrast, that what has happened is quite the reverse, according to real, critical, documented history? Why does this Castilian-Spanish nationalism ignore the errors it has made over the course of history or, if it does not ignore them, why does it not confess to them? Not to pamper Catalan nationalism, but so that those who suffer these miscon-ceptions may be duly informed and, as a logical result, eradicate this sad pernicious anti-Catalan syndrome, if not once and for all, at least gradually. Why is there no effort made from within Castilian culture to do something serious and in goodwill? For example, in the teaching of the history of Spain and Catalonia, in political education, in courses on journalism and when any opportunity presents itself – anything that would help to end this state of affairs, which has most certainly done no good and has led to so much pain. God alone knows how far it could go.

Maybe we live in the city happily and confidently in the certain belief that this 'anti-Catalan' syndrome is necessary for the good of Spain, because it reinforces Spanish patriotism and proves a tasty morsel or lure for picking up votes in certain political situa-tions? Or do people believe that perpetrating dislike and hatred down through the ages and throughout a lifetime is some kind of social virtue? Why does this aversion to everything Catalan survive endlessly century after century? Why is there not more interest shown in making this attitude disappear? Why is there no dialogue about this apparently conscious duty many people feel they have to demonstrate animosity towards Catalonia? Would it be possible to write and publish a book, as a serious, historical critique, that described the real motives behind such a suspicious, firmly entrenched tradition? It is a tradition which stokes enmity and hatred towards Catalonia and when it explodes, helped by the awe-inspiring power of press and televi-sion, it results in the pearls of wisdom we have seen, heard and read over the last few months. Is Catalonia the only country that does not merit dialogue, but insult instead, from groups of people whose concepts of nationalism lack learning and seriousness? I believe a book of this kind would perform a praiseworthy service to many Spanish-speaking citizens for, at least, they would know whether their anti-Catalan sympathies were really based on truth or on other motives.

What pleases and what offends about Spain

Therefore, my Spanish-speaking brothers, to elaborate on the reply to the question posed above – whether the person writing this is anti-Spanish or holds any animosity towards Spain – you have read what I think and, to a certain extent, I have explained myself. I am not anti-Spanish. I respect and love Spain and my prayers are with her. For the present and the future, I hope Spain will prosper in all senses and in good ways. My dream is for her nationalities and regions to live in perfect peace – a peace that comes from mutual respect for their values and historical rights, from the justness of their relationships and, especially, from love, however great or small, which is the origin of all true goodness.

As for Spain, there is only one reality that the Catalans do not like, that Catalans do not accept, that is bad for Catalans, and which many Spaniards living in Catalonia for some time, and like it here, are also known to dislike. It is the phenomenon – inexplicable and poorly studied, unpleasant yet nevertheless experienced by a large number of Spanish-speaking citizens – regarding the obsession or phobia against Catalonia, and almost solely against Catalonia, the 'anti-Catalan' syndrome with all its terrible consequences. Spain, with all that is good and fair about it, yes. Catalonia, with all that is good and fair about it, yes. The anti-Catalan syndrome or phobia, no.

To summarise my answer

Now, to summarise my answer to the above question, and to make sure the central idea is absolutely clear, as a Catalan citizen who wants to be reasonable and well-balanced, and because I am a Christian, I would like to stress that I have no phobia whatsoever against Spain. I love the Castilian-Spanish nationality and admire all the values that underlie, form and accredit it as distinct from the other nationalities in the state. I love and respect all the Spanish-speaking territories of Spain, both those belonging to Castile itself and the others. And, obviously, I love all the countries of the world because they are made up of people loved by God.

I accept Spanish nationalism and respect it as an expression of patriotism which, naturally, loves, preserves, defends and improves on its national values: the true wealth, inheritance and heritage of all its people embracing all spheres of culture, religion, tradition, etc. In other words, a fair, peaceful nationalism that coherently loves and respects the character and values of other nationalities. I do not know if historians would mention the times of Carlos I as an example, when there were no major problems with Catalonia and there was respect for its national customs, institutions and forms of self-government, times that are fondly remembered by Catalans. To this point, it is all natural and ethical, and is valid for all types of normal, defensive nationalism.

In the natural order of things, nationalism loses its equilibrium, reasonableness and validity when: it goes beyond the natural boundaries of enjoying and defending its own character and values and becomes an aggressor towards the national values of others, against their will, and takes recourse in power and violence; when nationalism attempts, in any way it sees fit and with all the means in its power, to completely change the character and customs of the other nation through assimilation, standardisation and destruction, however it is able. Any well-informed Catalan, who follows current events and the problems and phobias that accompany them, will not accept this kind of nationalism. He will expect the best possible form of progress, one that is fair, reasonable, peaceful and democratic, that works towards the benefit of all.

State Nationalism Tends not to Consider Itself a Form of Nationalism

The Spanish state seen from the standpoint of a state nationalist

The view held by a state nationalist of the Spanish state seems to be as follows: Spain is a single nation constituted as a state, with its own national characteristics (in reality, those of the Castilian nation), which must be held and understood as the only ones, because the unity and integrity of the state requires and demands it. Consequently, the existence and persistence of other national characteristics should not and cannot be permitted.

Hence the tendency, particularly from a certain date onwards, for the state to denigrate, persecute and seek to destroy any national characteristics that it has not adopted itself. In other words, instead of a diverse variety of values that enrich, it imposes uniformity, assimilates and absorbs which leads only to impoverishment. Instead of creating union, which brings unity with no disturbance or insult (which is possible), it establishes an absolute, repressive unity which, in fact, not only is unable to create harmony, it actually brings disintegration or, what to all intents and purposes is the same, demands not unity but uniformity. As a result, those who conceive state nationalism differently are seen as dangerous separatists who merit harsh disciplinary treatment, especially if they express or advocate different national convictions or sentiments. In these circum-stances it is no surprise that, as a normal, spontaneous measure of self-protection, defensive nationalism emerges, in this case Catalan nationalism, calmly and firmly defending national values that have been attacked in a variety of ways by the methods and resources of state nationalism.

There is a tendency not to call this type of state nationalism 'nationalism', out of habit and for suspicious reasons that lead to this habit. In contrast, the selfsame desire to defend, love and cultivate Catalan values is called 'nationalism' in the pejorative sense.

Recognising truth

It is important for truths to be recognised and expressed through dialogue in order to review certain pseudo-truths that harm the peaceful coexistence of different peoples. Acceptance must be sought for the rights of different groups and their corresponding duties, according to the case, not simply in name but an accep-tance that is profound and true – and perhaps even ecclesiastical. It should be achieved with the greatest possible respect for the individual (even, dare I say in fun, the Catalan individual).

Using these and other similar medicines, I hope and believe that these sick relationships can and will be cured as they should, judging by the events we have witnessed this year [1994] in the campaign against the national culture of Catalonia.

Something that is beyond explanation in our times

What has recently occurred is beyond explanation.[3] It has upset us very much here in Catalonia and has even met with surprise abroad. We were already aware in Catalonia of the lengths to which the antagonism between Spanish and Catalan nationalism could go. It was nothing new, but with the advent of democracy, the new Constitution and the step forward taken by the State of the Autonomies we expected the situation to have improved. This has not proved so. Ugliness and unpleasantness have reared their heads once again during this onslaught: animosity, hatred, disdain, jibe and insult. The anti-Catalan epidemic is not being treated, and quite a few sectors of society seem to be more interested in perpetuating this situation than in helping it to disappear. In contrast, it is my desire to solve this pending problem. There has been quite enough lack of understanding, animosity and hatred! Error and wrong must be cured by dialogue and respect, with the rectification required by right, duty and, above all, love. And what about the ecclesiastical world, surely there are still Christians today? It seems – if only it were not so – that there are Catholics in Spain who are mindful to love as Christ loves us, with one exception: their Catalan brothers, who are apparently not brothers. Everyone is forgiven, even enemies, except Catalans who for centuries now have been neither loved, nor forgiven, and, it seems, nor should they be according to certain people and groups, because their national conscience is different.

Is it because they are all seen as separatists? I believe many people think so. And I have every reason to believe it. There is so much factual and anecdotal evidence! The most widespread opinion in Catalonia is, I believe, that the small number of people who support independence do so, not because of Catalan nationalism, but as a result of the Spanish nationalism I am describing. Absurd? No. History clearly shows whether

---

[3]See note 2, above.

Catalonia has persecuted what the Castilian nation values or, in contrast, whether the nationalism of the Spanish state has, for centuries, with varying degrees, persecuted what the Catalan nation values. If a radical nationalist were to reply, as many have done in varying ways, 'Gentlemen, there are no national values or Catalan nationality involved here, just provinces and inhabitants who are always rebellious and hate Spain', if this were the case, then there would be no solution possible.

Second Overview: Specific Questions and Answers

Is the Person Writing a Nationalist?

I am a Catalan nationalist

I shall reply to another plausible question. Is the person writing a Catalan nationalist? Answer: I am a Catalan, above all, because I was born in and normally live in Catalonia. My parents, grand-parents and so on were also Catalan. To me this is of no special merit, but something Providence has given me for which I am grateful.

I am a Catalan nationalist, because I understand Catalan nationalism to be what I have described, and I consider it to be the most reasonable form. I am a nationalist because I love my native land: I value, love and defend the character and values it embraces, I personify it as a nation, and differentiate it from other natural nations that also enjoy their own distinct typical customs and values. I am a nationalist, but I do not suffer from overblown self-pride or disparage and despise the values of other nations. I am a nationalist who, as a result of natural reasoning and Christian imperative, loves and respects all nations, together with their people and the typical values and customs they love and defend. I am a nationalist who has attempted to examine and base the reasons for his arguments on good sources, not on foregone conclusions or prejudice, or out of political pressure, or because of other people's beliefs (in all modesty, I do not believe myself to be misinformed or ill-read). I am a whole-hearted Catalan nationalist: in other words my nationalism does not permit sentiments that could hurt others or hinder me in my duty as a Christian to love all people and all nations in the world.

I am saddened by the lack of brotherly love caused by indifference

It hurts and saddens me to see people and groups who, judging by their statements and behaviour, despite being Christians fail to love, or perhaps even hate, brothers who do not share their views on nationalism. I am a Catalan nationalist because, as a Catalan who very much loves what God has given me as both a person and citizen (not granted by nation or state), I have had to suffer quite a lot throughout my life because of the desires and intentions of others to take this away from me and wipe it out in my native land. They do not know what this suffering feels like because they have not experienced it. Their natural, just nationalism has not been attacked by another's nationalism, and they have not experienced persecution. I wish to add no more than one other reason: I am a nationalist Catalan because I do not believe that God has created people or groups with their own, distinct character and customs just so that other more powerful groups do with them as they see fit, with the right to ignore, standardise, assimilate or destroy, as there is no real objective need to do this in order to establish good, fair and loving cohabitation, within our differences. I am certain that to live together there must be other proper forms of 'brother–brother' relationships, instead of the 'master–servant' relationship found in aggressive nationalism, or 'foreigner–foreigner' in independence, which may be unnecessary and only brought about by the abuses of aggressive nationalism.

Possible evolution

Towards a model that does not create conflict between different nationalist groups

I hope and pray to God that what has been embarked upon in today's democracy, with the State of the Autonomies, may develop and meet greater challenges until a model is reached where conflicts between different nationalist groups, where one attacks another's values and the other is obliged to defend them, no longer exist. 'Exacerbated' nationalism should not exist, the present Pope has said. On my table I have The Liturgy of the Hours which contains the Church's official daily prayers and, from time to time, among others, we say a prayer: 'May those who hold the destiny of people in their hands, care not only for the well-being of their own nation, but also respect others and think too of other peoples'. This does not sound aggressive or exacerbated: it emanates love, which is what is lacking in all human conflict between individuals or groups.

Can we expect a change?

Looking ahead to a better tomorrow, can we expect the so-called State of the Autonomies, having taken the initial step, to progress towards fair, reasonable improvements and eventually reach an honourable state of affairs, where rights and values are restored, where state nationalism calls a definitive halt to its abuses, and non-state nationalism can feel well treated and satisfied? A good, peaceful, agreeable and fruitful coexistence having thus been created, thoughts of independence – not, as I say, the result of separatist sentiment but of separating influences – would no longer be tempting, necessary or inevitable.

If this positive change were to occur – I do not believe that there are many who would seriously consider what has been said about 'coffee for all',[2] because coffee really is for everyone and may be bought and sold, but the rights and values of each nationality or nation are not the same and are not the same thing to everyone, nor can they be bought and sold – the majority of traditional nationalists would probably believe that their rights had been satisfied and would not consider independence as the only, irremediable alternative. This positive evolution towards fairer conditions that lead to the greatest good and where national rights are fully guaranteed, without the risk of harm caused by sudden, ill-conceived change, is possible and desirable. What matters is that this change is brought about by lawful, effective means.

Isn't nationalism a whimsical notion?

A description of whimsical nationalism

Another question that could be posed is, isn't nationalism a

---

[2]Translator's note: The original Spanish expression, *'café para todos'*, is a sarcastic reference belittling the desire of various nationalities and regions in Spain to achieve autonomy.

somewhat whimsical notion? Won't we see a nationalism on every street corner and be obliged to acknowledge any group who feels inspired by or master of every new nationalism?

This is not difficult to answer so long as we have clear, well-understood and accepted concepts. It is not easy for a whimsical nationalism of this nature to arise, but we can imagine one in the following circumstances: in state X all the inhabitants speak a single, ancient language that has not been introduced from outside its frontiers. Given that only one common language has been spoken in this state, we do not see two cultures, nor are there two distinct histories, or any event that could cause division between citizens, except for the opinions of political ideologies and parties. All unite under the threat of major problems, such as foreign oppression, for example. There is only one nationalism because there is one single state resting on a single nationality or nation. There are no problems of plurinationality. However, we then find that one part of the uninational territory, for some new, special reason – due to some vanity, believing itself to more highly developed, or for whatever reason – falls into the temptation of wanting to form a separate group and constitute itself as a nation or something of the kind, in a simple desire for differentiation. It then proclaims itself as a nationalist group and forms a political party on the basis of this idea.

What would my readers say of this case? I suppose they would say that it was whimsical, and I completely agree. It is whimsical because it is not a natural situation, and it is not natural because the basic elements of nationality and nation are missing, the ones I repeat so often and which make up the 'differential factor': its own distinct language, distinct culture, distinct history, habits, particular institutions, etc.; the awareness and conviction to own these realities; the will to preserve them as wealth of one's own; and, with greater reason, a good recollection that – as in the Catalan case – these and other traditions and values have been maintained and experienced in freedom, free from opposition or persecution, in the past and that, at a given moment in history, they were unjustly persecuted and snatched away. In short, what I frequently call the characteristic and constituting values of a true nationality or nationhood.

A comparison between true and whimsical nationalism

In the case of whimsical nationalism just described these elements are missing. Not with non-whimsical nations and real, natural national groups however, whether they are nation-states or nations in a plurinational state, where these values are present and upheld. They are values that do not easily die because a superior force wants them to disappear.

I have a special reason for wanting to stress the difference between whimsical – and therefore not real, because it possesses no characteristic customs and values – and true, natural nationalism, which is sustained by these customs and values. Should any of my readers be confused on this point about nationalism or, what would be worse, be encouraged to think it is all story-tales, obsessions or tasteless capriciousness, I hope they calmly reflect, realise that nationalist groups really exist, that it is logical for them to exist and that they come in a variety of different colours. With this aim in mind, please see the following classification, which may help the reader to distinguish better between the different types of nationalism.

A digression on types of nationalist philosophies

Natural

This is nationalism that springs from the fair, sentimental and spiritual reactions of citizens, based on the historical roots, values and rights of their nationality. It is distinguished by the fact that its expression and manifestation is honourable, orderly and positive inside its own nation and – in its relationship to other nations or types of nationalism – its ways of thinking and courses of action are not exacerbated, unjust, overbearing or aggressive.

Whimsical

Excitedly arises from the enthusiasm of a human group because of specific ideas or factors, but is not based on the characteristic features of natural historical nations which normally create the types of nationalism we know; see the description given in foot-note 3 b, below.

Exacerbated

Internally: the hypertrophy of national values to the point where they are considered to be exemplary and the only ones of worth. Externally: instead of respecting other legitimate types of nationalism, it is unjust and becomes overbearing towards them, encroaching upon, subjugating and quashing their rights. It is blind and mute when it comes to dialogue. A specific nationalism may not necessarily be prone to all these defects but it could bring on one or several of them (see the comments on aggressive nationalism that follow). From the example and sad models of Soviet nationalism and German National Socialism to current less turbulent types of nationalism that operate by gentler, tactical yet effective means, this type embodies a wide variety of methods.

Aggressive

This is the previous exacerbated nationalism, but underscored in its *ad extra* component. One of its variants is the plurinational state that does not respect but instead disrupts, attacks or persecutes the nations, or nation, it contains within its territory in order to assimilate, absorb or standardise. The final goal is for the state to cease being plurinational and devote itself to creating a total, homogenous unity.[3]

---

[3]Regarding this type of negative nationalism – exacerbated *ad intra* and aggressive *ad extra* – Pius XII wrote the following for the previously mentioned 1954 Christmas broadcast (see Chaper Three note 1):

a) 'In essence the mistake consists of confusing *national life*, in its true sense, with *nationalist politics*: in the *former*, the right and honour of a people, can and should be championed; the *latter*, as the root of infinite evil, can never be sufficiently condemned.'

b) 'In itself, *national life* is the operating group of all the customs and values of civilisation that belong to and are characteristic of a specific group, and whose spiritual unity forms the bond. Also, by its own contributions, this life enhances the culture of all humanity. In its essence, therefore, *national life* is non-political, so that, as history and experience demonstrate, *it can grow together with others in the same State, as it can also extend beyond the political confines of the State.*'

c) '*National life* was not the cause of dissolution within the community of peoples, but only when it began to be used as a *means to political ends*. In other words, when the *dominant, centralist State* made nationalism the basis for its *expansive force*. This led to the birth of the *nationalist State, the source of rivalry and stimulus for discord.*'

(The division into sections and italics are mine. See, Collection of Encyclicals and Pontifical Documents, translation and indexes by Monsignor Pascual Galindo. Published by the Junta Técnica Nacional, Madrid, 1955).

Defensive

The concept and reality of defensive nationalism are clearly deduced from the concept and reality of aggressive nationalism. Defensive nationalism wishes to live its own life in freedom and is not interested in encroaching upon what historically and ethically belongs to other nations. It will not permit its character and values to be replaced by those a stronger nation is imposing or wishes to impose. If its values are not attacked, it minds its own business and respects the business of others. If attacked, especially if the oppression is secular and enduring, it defends itself ethically, lawfully and peacefully, using non-violent and honest ways and means. It believes that violence and arms are not the ideal run-of-the-mill or ethical means to sort out human rights problems, whether of individuals or groups.[4]

Law abiding

In calm control   The situation may, and does, arise where a citizen lives in a plurinational state whose nationalism is, in fact, exacerbated and which treats the nation or nations forming part of its territory unjustly. The education this citizen has received in his schooling, what has been passed down from his parents, the environment in which he lives and state laws, have distorted how he thinks and so he is not aware that his type of nationalism, exaggerated as it is by opinions, attitudes and behaviour, is in total accord with the nationalism of the state and with all the ways it is expressed and imposed by law, education and propaganda, etc. He experiences, without being aware of it, an exacerbated nationalism, not because of passion but because of inertia. This man, who would probably reproach citizens of other non-state nationalities for having suspicious or wayward attitudes towards state nationalism, when asked for his opinion, would say, 'I obey the laws of the state. The law sets the rules and guidelines of social and political life. My nationalism is law abiding. The views of those who disagree with the laws of the state do not convince or worry me, in fact they annoy me.' And he will be perfectly happy with that.

---

[4]See Chapter 3, note 3.

But in an unfortunate situation   He may be happy, perhaps; but his happiness is not based on proper reasoning. There are probably many citizens who carry on in this way, but they are wrong. They confuse law abiding with truth and goodness, when in fact these things cannot and should not be confused, because they are different. Not everything that is lawful is true and good, and neither is everything that is true and good lawful. There can be bad laws, and they exist. Were the cruel laws of the communist Soviet regime, to give an example, all good? Innumerable victims could answer that question. Were the laws of Nazi Germany all honest? Leaving aside dictatorships to look at the democracies of our days, are the laws that pronounce, defend and extend specific assumptions about voluntary abortion also good? Is it good, natural or loving for a woman to want and allow the child in her womb, not a tumour or beast but a person, a human life with all the dignity granted by God, to be delivered into the hands of a man and torn to pieces, the decision of both, mother and doctor, protected by a 'democratic' law?

Not all that is lawful is moral   What I am attempting to do here is to remind the reader that not all that is lawful is good, and that there are laws that are not beneficial for the common good of society; they do not respect rights, among others the right to life, and, in another vein, those affecting cultures and peoples. From this point onwards the individual must listen to his own conscience and ensure that he is duly informed and abide by, where possible, natural law and the law of the Gospel. The citizen should take good care to discern whether a law affecting nationalist issues has been drawn up by free, impartial men or by those committed to one side along with its injustices.

Is all well with Catalan nationalism?

I suspect that some reader might be saying, 'The text gives a harsh description of a supposedly aggressive, exacerbated nationalism, applied to the historical nationalism of the Spanish state. I do not remember seeing Catalan nationalism described, harshly or otherwise. Is all well here? Is there really nothing wrong?' It is a good question. We shall see if I get the answer right.

I think I have described the most important factors. Catalonia is a human group, within the Spanish state, which is endowed with valued characteristics: a distinct language and culture, the consciousness of being a nation and the will to continue as one. It has, therefore, the will and determination not to die out as a nation, even if it does not represent a state in its own right and exists within another state which has, for the last three centuries, rested on a nation with different characteristics. The latter has the peculiar feature that, intermittently and to a greater or lesser degree, it persecutes the above-mentioned characteristics with the aim, by wiping them out, of achieving absolute uniformity and eradicating conflict, where nationalism is concerned. Any further description is neither necessary or convenient, and I have deliberately shied away from this so as not to upset or give the impression that I am intent on attacking with lists of disagreeable events. This book is not the right place for a detailed account of regrettable, sad events. These events are more appropriately dealt with in history books, the text of which has already been written and is available to all; it is a pity that it is not duly known. I believe, therefore, that I have said enough about Catalan nationalism: nationalism exists because it is a natural historical nation that defends itself. That should be enough.

It is very natural and human for mistakes to have been made and ill-considered actions employed in the just defence of values. We are men, and all men and women can and do err, can and do sin, as a result of our human limitations. What I do believe I am right in suspecting is that in a human situation where the strongest attacks and the weakest defends itself, it is the strong who are more likely to suffer errors and commit reprehensible acts, than the weak who are the victims of the errors and actions perpetrated by the strong. As for the rest, history is the witness of both behaviours.

Are the assertions made by Catalan nationalists new?

It occurs to me that more than one reader may have a further objection which I should answer. Towards the end of this book, the view given of Spain in terms of nationalist philosophies is based on two assertions: Spain is a plurinational state; and Catalonia is a nation. Very well, these assertions have been voiced by Catalan nationalists for a relatively short time. It consists of a new, previously unheard of development.

Some background history

The difficulty in replying to this objection lies not in the concepts, but in how many lines I would need to express them. I'll try to be brief. When I was a child or pre-adolescent I also had no idea what a plurinational state was, or a nationality, or precisely what Spain and Catalonia were. However, I did possess the sentiments of a member of a nation, although I would not have been able to describe them adequately. I knew that in Catalonia we spoke the Catalan language (though we were assured that it was only a dialect), while in other places they spoke another language, Spanish. Specifically, in our towns we always spoke Catalan and it struck one to hear Spanish being spoken.

Gradually, the media of those days and my studies helped me to understand the scene with increasing clarity. The definition of concepts grew. The renaissance of Catalan culture, begun the century before, had taken very important steps. Poets, artists, politicians, publications, etc., corroborated the fact that this 'something', which produced a variety of words like region, country, nationality, etc., fully deserved the name of nation, even though it lacked a state. Finally, its existence was revindicated with the Statute of Autonomy, the Catalan differential factor was recognised and the concepts clarified.

I say 'the Catalan differential factor was recognised and the concepts clarified', but I have not been accurate. I doubt that the Catalan factor will ever become clear to exacerbated Spanish nationalists, or others who may not be so radical but are still infected with the famous 'anti-Catalan phobia'.

The Position of the Spanish Constitution of 1978

Preamble

Fortunately, however, something has changed over time and, as proof, I quote the Constitution in force.[5] From the preamble: 'to

---

[5]The italics here, and in the extracts which follow, are mine.

protect all *Spaniards and peoples* of Spain in the (...) exercise of their *human rights, their cultures and traditions, languages and institutions'*. During the days when Spanish nationalism was more shrill, these radicals would berate a Catalan who spoke his own language in the following way, 'Speak Christian, Sir!' It was spoken in bad taste, but not in order to hurt. Whoever behaved this way believed himself to be a normal Spaniard setting an example to a Catalan nationalist (nationalist in the pejorative sense), without noticing that, really, the exacerbated nationalist was precisely himself, while the Catalan was a normal, non-aggressive, if not defensive, nationalist. In contrast, and it is enjoyable to confirm it, the Constitution in recognition of modern times protects the Catalan language and its culture, which have been harassed for centuries by those who mistakenly thought that, by persecuting or killing off the language and culture of Catalonia, they would be enhancing Spanish culture.

Preliminary heading, second article

The Constitution continues with the preliminary heading, article 2: 'The Constitution is based on the indissoluble unity of the Spanish nation, common and indivisible country of all Spaniards, and recognises and guarantees *the right to autonomy of the nationalities and regions* that integrate it and solidarity between them all'. The step forward taken by the Constitution in recognising the nationalities seems clear. Classical Spanish nationalism did not recognise them, and still less did it guarantee them. However, a Catalan who knows his history and the events of these last few months should not think he is offending anyone just because he suspects that many non-Catalan nationalists do not recognise this right, or dislike the Constitution recognising and guaranteeing it. As for the indissoluble unity of Spain, I have already said, and it is well known, that unity is one thing (which can crystallise in a variety of ways, in both religion and civil order), and another is uniform, assimilating and absorbing sameness, which neither respects the human rights of the individual nor nations.

Preliminary heading, third article, two and three

The text continues (article 3,2): 'The other Spanish *languages* shall also be *official* in their respective communities in accordance with their statutes.' Also remember that classical Spanish nationalism, especially during the dictatorships, did not admit the official or co-official status of the languages of Spain and, what is worse, did not want them to exist – in fact, quite the opposite.

I continue. Article 3,3: 'The wealth of the distinct *linguistic types* in Spain is a cultural heritage that shall be the object of special *respect and protection.*' What did aggressive, classical Spanish nationalists think then, and what do they think now, about this 'wealth' that defensive nationalists have always valued so much? I finish my quotes from the Spanish Constitution with this one from article 10,1 and 2: 'The dignity of the individual, the inherent inviolable rights, *the free development of nationality*, respect for the law and the rights of others are the *foundations of public order and social peace.*'

Further down, the following important clarification is added: 'The laws regarding the fundamental rights and freedoms recognised by the Constitution shall be interpreted in accordance with the *Universal Declaration of Human Rights* and *international treaties* and *agreements* on these subjects, ratified by Spain' (...)

I believe that this is enough in the way of a reply to the proposed objection. The meanings of nationality, nation and plurinationality, etc., have already been described in previous pages.

Is there any point to the 'national day of Catalonia'?

A holiday is held in Catalonia which perhaps not many understand, and those who live exacerbated Spanish nationalism with intensity not only do not understand it, but they are bound to have a poor view of it and consider it to be an affront to Spain. This day commemorates 11 September 1714, when, after a resistance lasting thirteen months during the final chapters of a war that had gone on for nine years, the city of Barcelona fell to the troops of Felipe V, led by the Duke of Berwick. The Duke then immediately proceeded to dissolve the *Generalitat* (government of Catalonia) and the Municipal Council and, in their place, set up the Superior Board of Justice and Governance, and a Provisional Board of sixteen administrators for the municipality. Subsequently, in 1716, a newly presented Royal Decree replaced the *Decree* dictated by the previous autonomous government.

The public holiday currently commemorated in Catalonia is not an affront or attack on Spain; it is simply a calm, firm and peaceful act which asserts Catalan nationality, and all the corresponding attributes of language and culture; a historical, rich, unrelinquishable nationality that the people wish to preserve in peace, because it is theirs, and represents no disservice or aggression towards other nationalities.

This holiday, which Catalans call *la Diada*, recalls a very sad date, but the majority of Catalans do not gather solely in vindication – apart from a few exceptions. They celebrate the positive side much more, setting their sights on what is good and can be improved upon in Catalonia and Spain. As I have said, it would be incomparably better to have a Spain of brothers, where the various nationalities and regions could live together in love and respect, leaving abuse and injustice behind, rather than a Spain where, as the result of a historical defeat such as the one recalled on this day, these conditions would hardly be met. As long as this negative disposition persists in Spain, we will continue to have serious problems which might otherwise be avoided, and peace and true unity will not be possible, just a falsely imposed peace and artificial unity. These are serious problems, as I say, which will, if they are not sorted out properly, not only be troublesome and harmful for Catalonia – which they already have been – but also for Spain, which no one is likely to want.

How does true nationalism respond to the Third and Fourth Worlds?

While on the subject of problems, and bearing in mind the recent International Conference On Population and Development held in Cairo, I cannot help referring to the terrible situation of social injustice which people in the so-called 'First World' contribute towards creating. The 'rich' squander vast amounts of money, which are completely unnecessary for leading an honest, reasonable life, wasting it on superfluous luxuries, vanities, vices, sumptuous and ostentatious lifestyles, and a long list of passing whims that are neither necessary nor advisable. It disregards so many millions of brothers living in the so-called 'Third' and 'Fourth' Worlds teeming with all the imaginable, and unimaginable, kinds of poverty and misery possible. This enormously cruel injustice is an old one, but it is now more widely recognised, and it is easy and reprehensible to perpetrate it.

Perhaps God has created two worlds, one for those who have the right to go on squandering their money on pleasures, and another for the rest, who must live a life of suffering, deprived of basic necessities and dying of hunger? God has created goods so that we all use what is necessary, not for some to squander and waste, while others perish from starvation. The love ordained for our nations, who are clothed and fed and – except in the Fourth World – have what they need, is good in itself. However, precisely because it is fair and honest, because it is genuinely human, this love is only as good as it proves itself to be by opening up and showing more and more compassion for nations where the majority of the people live in subhuman conditions.

While some, due to complex circumstances, are born to live in misery, the fair, human – and above all Christian – thing is for those who are not living in poverty, and have abundantly sufficient resources, to be loving and just and help those who are, so that they are not forced to live and die 'today' by the wayside, but instead learn to help themselves and avoid poverty 'tomorrow'. Effective aid to poor countries is the best badge of true nationalism, the type that loves other nations as it does its own.

EPILOGUE

Peace

Do not forget that the author is not a politician, or someone wanting to stoke controversy, bitterness or resentment against all that is Castilian or Spanish. I am an ordinary man in the street, a Christian and a bishop who loves one and all. I am a man of peace and therefore no partisan to war, violence or injustice. I am a Catalan who loves the land, people and values of Catalonia, which does not mean I dislike or do not love other lands, people or different values. I am a man who is fully aware that, when it comes to human problems, you must always love and respect people, because this is the law of God; and you must distinguish them from their deeds and misdoings which publicly cause harm to other people, the victims of these acts. This is where I stand. I fervently hope that the many fellow citizens who suffer from the 'anti-Catalan syndrome' can free themselves from its hold, symptoms which perpetuate an ancient disease which no therapy has yet managed to eradicate.

Love and Dialogue

If we are to get over this disease, I implore society to abandon these failed secular treatments once and for all, and replace them with ones that offer the only effective hope: proper information about the disease and its causes and effects; a climate of peace, no slur campaigns or tasteless jibes; open, respectful dialogue, not a dialogue of the deaf or shouting matches; nor a dialogue between judges and offenders, but between brothers, individuals and children of God; and last, but not least, a great deal of love.

If we are not able to treat the disease – totally or partially – with these or similar remedies, the anti-Catalan syndrome will not go away. And I repeat, for the benefit of the followers of Jesus Christ and His teachings: Brothers, do you believe that stirring and keeping this anti-Catalan phobia alive as a national tradition obeys Christ's precious order to 'Love one another as I have loved you'? The duty to love one's fellow man cannot be ignored in any walk of life, and is consequently equally valid when applied to nationalism, whether it is just and defensive, or unjust and aggressive.

Without love we cannot live or live together. Where there is a persistent sediment of animosity, it is impossible to see reason or think and analyse why a phobia is accepted, allowed and sustained. By getting rid of animosity, many windows will open to help discern the full force and truth of the issues in the light of day, and provide reasonable solutions, including the courage to recognise where one may have gone wrong.

The constitutional factor, whose positive declarations I have stressed, and the real difficulties for life in the autonomies – to differing degrees of awareness and content – to be seen throughout the state, can be interpreted with optimism and offer the first steps towards a solution whose fulfilment I wholeheartedly desire for the good of all nationalities and regions in the state.

A Plea for Calm Reflection

We need to be better informed on the histories of Spain and Catalonia, initiate proper discussion, and humbly and reasonably ask extreme Spanish nationalists to question their convictions that all is well, that they are always right, and that in Spain there is only one kind of nationalism, the rebellious, dangerous and unpleasant kind found in four provinces that 'do not want to be Spanish', 'Spanish' meaning something that is assumed to be incompatible with Catalan nationalism.

From Re-examination to Co-operation

Although I could say more , brothers and friends, than I have written here, I now close my notes. My kind regards to all. To those of you suffering from the 'anti-Catalan syndrome', I ask you to be generous and re-examine your attitudes and views. To those of you who show Catalans the same love and respect that you show your brothers in other nations and regions in Spain, I greet you not only with equal love and respect, but also with admiration as your integrity is no small thing and deserves considerable gratitude. I ask all of you to contribute towards rationalising our ideas and attitudes to the various forms of nationalism, because mistaken and negative behaviour is the root of much evil.

Till we meet again in heaven where, as I have said elsewhere, there are no nations or nationalism of any kind, but a new land where justice and love live for evermore.

Vic, 15 September 1994
Feast of Our Lady of Sorrows

N.B. Having finished these notes addressed to my Spanish-speaking brothers, it occurs to me that I should also invite my brothers who speak Catalan and other languages throughout Spain to read them too.

POSTSCRIPT

To my Spanish-speaking Brothers Living in Catalonia

What I have written so far is addressed to all my Spanish-speaking brothers without exception. It is understood, however, that, though I have no intention of excluding anyone, given the particular nature of the debate, it would be of less importance to those in the Americas, who have their own problems and circumstances.

If anything in particular needs to be added, apart from what I have already said for the benefit of all, it is to the residents of Catalonia, especially those who have shared their daily lives with their Catalan-speaking brothers for many years. I feel duty bound out of courtesy to add a few words for their benefit.

To this end, it occurs to me to include a fragment from my book *El problema Català* (The Catalan Problem) which I have already quoted in the pages above. I think it is appropriate in this context.

'The problems of the working world in our country complicate the Catalan problem to a certain extent, bearing in mind the large number of people from other areas of Spain who live in Catalonia. These people work and it is natural enough for them to be more concerned with earning their daily bread than anything which may appear political to them and, therefore, secondary. Furthermore, they come from particular communities in the peninsula where the view held of the Catalan problem is not usually one of sympathy or understanding, with the odd exception. They come from places where the people, because of general opinion, their education or by tradition, are clearly in favour of assimilating centralism. The tradition they know does not go back more than three centuries, but they probably believe that the situation has always been like this.

'These brothers live with us, and some feel at home and already have children and families here, loving the land that has welcomed and helped them. Some of these people not only understand Catalonia but also think of themselves as passionate Catalans. However, not everyone thinks this way, and differences in opinion could hinder hopes for a serious Catalan identity forging ahead, because the immigration factor and circumstances surrounding it could, to a certain extent, hamper progress.

'Immigration is a serious fact, and against facts reasons count for little. It is important, therefore, to understand and appreciate this properly, and to extract as much on the positive angle from it as we can. The future should be reflected upon, deliberating with the right attitude to reach proper answers, honestly and efficiently rectifying the parts that do not work. Our non-Catalan brothers living alongside us, *els altres catalans* (the other Catalans), should have a good understanding of Catalonia such as it is, put aside any prejudice they may have, and work as the locals do to head the country in the direction well-informed Catalans are aiming at. Specific solutions? These are goods my shop does not stock. Whatever I could say as a Christian Catalan and a member of the Church hierarchy I have already said elsewhere. Other fields – in the lay world – intellectuals, artists, teachers, businessmen, governors, unions and the media, should realise it is important to work for a better atmosphere, both in terms of social justice (achieved not through revolution but through faster rational evolution than has been undertaken to date), and in terms of the non-Catalans living in Catalonia.

'In so far as the latter is concerned, it is important to create a perfect example of peaceful coexistence, politeness and respect, and no discrimination of any kind, so that immigrants feel comfortable living with us, not resentful because of some rude or ill behaviour on the part of a fellow Catalan, and so that exemplary civility and Christian brotherhood reign in all circumstances. As for fellow citizens from other countries, it is important to remind them, in the right way – through schooling etc. – that they should treat us in the same way. They should bear in mind that all immigration, foreign or domestic, is based on a principle whereby the immigrant should be highly esteemed and respected, but he must also reciprocate these sentiments, without expecting privileges, sincerely adapting to what he finds and not imposing his point of view over and above the reasonable attitudes of the natives. He should try to fit in, stand up for his rights, not create unnecessary conflicts and do nothing that might cause the impression he is in any way ungrateful to the country that has welcomed him. There is nothing humiliating about behaving in this way, nor does it betray an inferiority complex: it is an honourable, elegant way to behave. I have brought to the fore two closely related problems that require considerable clarity, sacrifice and understanding. It is best not to get embroiled in utopian or overexcited and emotional babbling which contributes nothing positive, and not to let reason seep away through the crevices in rash carelessness. If we really want things to go well, like it or not, we need to solve the problems.'

Having said this, I cannot express affection for you as my much-loved Spanish-speaking brothers – the 'other Catalans' as a writer put so well in Catalan, though his native tongue was Spanish – in any better way than to hope that your lives in Catalonia may be happy, that you share our joys with us and bear too the burdens and setbacks which life and cohabitation bring us all, especially in these arduous times of crisis.

There is also something special I beg of you: to work for the prosperity of Catalonia, in all its facets, material and economic; for social justice, peace and goodwill; for courtesy, responsibility and understanding in politics; and to take an active part in restoring and improving religious and moral values, which have fallen so low in both your land and ours – which saddens me, especially here in Catalonia – because if these things fail us, so will everything else. I think that many of you feel the same. Prosperity on all sides, in your land and ours, is the best thing to wish and pray for from God, and the best possible gift we could desire for Spain.

And one last thing, hopefully it is the last. Something that I

believe many other Catalans also think, and I suggest in the way
of advice: should anyone in Catalonia, angered by the anti-
Catalan campaigns led by certain media, make some disagreeable remark which before this campaign he would not normally
have made – your humble servant has received no news of such
a case – please keep your temper and contribute to peace in your
own way. Once the storm has blown over, I am sure there will
be better times to come. To those who persist in harbouring
such bitterness against us, if it is in your power, ask them to
change their attitude and, if you think it is fair and sensible to
do so, suggest they stop talking about something they probably
know nothing about, and that they come to Catalonia with a
little goodwill and stay for a while. Brothers: to those of you
who live here with us, and to us all, we need prosperity and
peace. Farewell.

DOCUMENTS FROM THE MAGISTERIUM OF THE CHURCH

Out of the abundant documentation held by the Magisterium of the Church on the subject of nationalities and ethnic minorities I have selected the following texts closely related to the message of my book. I wholeheartedly recommend they should be read.

Speech given by Pope John Paul II to UNESCO (2 June 1980)

On 2 June 1980, Pope John Paul II visited UNESCO headquarters and gave a memorable speech.

After referring to the inalienable rights of man in his introduction, he presents two fundamental concepts. In the first he deals with man as the primordial and fundamental subject, object, purpose and achievement of culture. In the second, after outlining certain facets of the relationships between the above institution and the Church, he exhaustively analyses the cross-currents between the gospel and mankind. Having defined the concepts, he proceeds to draw some conclusions of paramount importance. He begins by asserting that the first role of culture is to educate the individual, the family and the school system, by centring on a sense of 'being greater' in keeping with the poorly and hardly ever satisfied demands of human dignity. At this point, he continues with the following concepts (numbers 14 and 15):

'14. If, in the name of the future of culture, we must assert man's right to "be" greater, and if by the same token we must demand a healthy primacy of the family as part and parcel of educating mankind along the road to true humanity, we must then also put the rights of nations on the same footing; we must lay them down as the basis of culture and education.

'In effect the nation is a large community of people united by a variety of ties but, above all, precisely by culture. The nation exists "because of" culture and "for" culture. Culture, therefore, is the great educator of men so that they may "be greater" within the community. Culture possesses a history which goes beyond the history of the individual and the family. It is also within the community, the basis upon which all families educate, that the family begins the task of teaching the simplest thing, language, so that man from his early beginnings learns to speak and become a member of the community which is his family and nation.

'In all that I proclaim here, and I shall continue to do so to my utmost, my words convey a personal experience, a personal testimony of a sort. I am the son of a nation that has lived through some of the greatest events of history, whose neigh-bours have repeatedly condemned to death, but has survived and kept its personality. It has preserved its identity and, despite division and invasion by foreigners, has preserved its national sovereignty, not by relying on physical strength, but only by relying on its culture. In this case, culture seems to be endowed with a greater power than all other forces. Therefore, when I refer to the right of nationhood on the basis of culture and future, it finds no echo with "nationalism", it is at all times a stable component of the human experience and of the prospects for man's development along humanist lines.

'There is a fundamental sovereignty in the society that mani-fests itself in the culture of a nation. This is the sovereignty where man is also supremely sovereign. When I speak this way, I also think, with deep inner-felt emotion, of the cultures of so many ancient peoples who have not given ground when confronted by invader civilisations. They persist to this day for mankind as a source of man's "being" at the true root of human-ity. In admiration, I also think of the cultures of the new soci-eties, that spring to life within the community of the nation itself – just as my nation sprang to life ten centuries ago – and struggle to maintain their identity and values in the face of the influences and pressures of models from outside.

'15. By addressing you, ladies and gentlemen, who have gathered here for over 30 years in the name of man's cultural pre-eminence, communities, peoples and nations, I say to you: with all the means at your disposal keep watch over this fundamental sovereignty that each nation possesses by virtue of its culture. Protect it like a child who is the apple of your eye for the future good of our large human family. Protect it! Do not let this fundamental sovereignty become prisoner to any political or financial interest. Do not let it fall victim to totalitarianism, imperialism or hegemony, where man only features as an object of domination and not as the subject of his own existence. In their shadow even a nation – their own and other nations – only features as bait for various interests and is an object of domination, not the subject: the subject of a sovereignty arising from a genuine culture that belongs to it as property. Surely one could not claim that there are no nations, on the face of Europe or the world, with a marvellous historical sovereignty that arises from their culture which are, nevertheless, also deprived of their full sovereignty? Is this not an important question for the future of human culture, especially important in our times, when it is so urgent to eliminate the remains of colonialism?'

The remaining conclusions affect the communications media, literacy, and the rights of the Church in education, the universities and specialised institutions. The Pope closes his speech by elaborating on certain thoughts about scientific research, the threat hovering over the future of the world and the mobilisation of conscience.

Message read by Pope John Paul II on World Peace Day: 'Respect Minorities and Build Peace' (1 January 1989)

On 1 January, 1989, Pope John Paul II published a message entitled, 'Respect Minorities and Build Peace' on the occasion of World Peace Day.[1]

The introduction presents the subject of minorities as a delicate, urgent question and describes their vastly different conditions in various societies across the planet. He then reminds his audience of two fundamental principles: dignity (of the human being and human groups) and unity (of the family).

On the subject of the dignity of human groups, we read the following:

'[Human groups] have the right to their collective identity which needs to be fostered according to the dignity of each one of its members. This right is immutable even in cases where the group, or some of its members, acts against the common good. In these cases the presumed unlawful action needs to be examined by the responsible authority without condemning the group as a whole, as this goes against justice. In their turn, members of minorities have a duty to treat others with the same respect and sense of dignity'.

On the subject of the unity of the human family, we are reminded that:

'It has its origins in a single God and creator who, according to Holy Scripture, "hath made of one blood all nations of men for to dwell on all the face of the earth" (Acts of the Apostles 17, 26). The unity of the human race means that all humanity, beyond its various ethnic, national, cultural and religious divisions, constitutes one community, free of discrimination between peoples, that leans to reciprocal solidarity. Unity also requires the diversity of the human family to serve the consolidation of this unity, instead of creating division.'

The text continues by reminding us of the obligation to accept

---

[1] I have inserted headings to aid the reader of this speech.

and foster diversity. This pertains to the state, groups and each individual.

'An open, clear mind, wishing to reach a better understanding of the cultural heritage of the minorities with whom it mixes, will help eliminate the prejudiced behaviour that hinders healthy relations. This is a process that requires constant monitoring as, very often, similar behaviour will appear under new forms.'

The speech then moves on to specify the rights and duties of minorities in a democracy.

Rights:

a) *The right to exist*: 'The first right of minorities is the right to exist. This right may be ignored in a variety of ways, even to the extreme of it being denied by clear or indirect forms of genocide. The right to life, as such, is an inalienable right, and a state that persecutes or tolerates acts that puts the lives of citizens from minorities in danger violates a fundamental law that regulates social order. The right to exist can also suffer harm by more subtle forms. Some peoples, in particular those classified as native or aborigine, have always had a special relationship with their land, which is intimately linked to their identity and tribal, cultural and religious traditions. When indigenous populations are deprived of their land, they lose a vital component of their existence and run the risk of disappearing as a people.'

b) *The right to defend and pursue one's own culture*: 'Another right that must be safeguarded is the right of minorities to defend and pursue their own culture. It is not uncommon to find minority groups in danger of cultural extinction. In fact, some places have adopted legislation which does not recognise the right to use one's own language. Sometimes, changes of family and place names have also been imposed. On certain occasions minorities have seen their artistic and literary expressions ignored, and lack sufficient space in public life for their holidays and other celebrations. All this may lead to the loss of a rich cultural inheritance.'

c) *The right of relating to groups of common cultural and historical inheritance*: 'This right is closely linked to maintaining relations with groups that have a common cultural and historical inheritance but live in the territories of other states.'

d) *The right to religious freedom*: 'Here I will only make a brief reference to the right to religious freedom, as it was already the subject of the Message for World Peace Day last year. This is a right which in addition to individuals affects all religious communities, and includes all free demonstrations of one's religious convictions, both individual and collective. This means that minorities have the legal power to communally celebrate their own rituals. These minorities should be able to offer religious education using the style of teaching they find most appropriate, and employing the necessary means. Furthermore, it is important that the state effectively guarantees and promotes the fostering of religious freedom, particularly when, in addition to a large majority of believers from a specific religion, there are one or more minority groups belonging to other faiths. Finally, minority religions should be guaranteed the fair freedom of exchange and relationships with other communities, both inside and outside national borders.'

These rights should be the aim not just of understanding but also, and above all, of assimilation. With respect to this point, we read the following:

'The fundamental rights of the individual have been endorsed in modern times by various national and international documents. Essential as these legal instruments are, they are nevertheless insufficient to overcome deeply ingrained prejudice and suspicion, or eliminate ways of thinking that inspire reactions against members of minority groups. The assimilation of law in human behaviour is a slow, deep-seated process, especially when it comes to eliminating this type of behaviour, however, that does not make the task any less urgent. Not just the state, every individual too is obliged to do whatever he can to attain this goal. The state, however, can play a significant role in encouraging cultural initiatives and exchanges to ease mutual understanding, as well as promoting educational programmes that help teach youngsters to respect others and reject prejudice, much of which is the result of ignorance. Parents also have a great deal of responsibility, as children learn a lot through observation and are likely to adopt their parents' views on other peoples and groups.

'There is little doubt that the pursuit of a culture based on respect for others is essential for building a peaceful society. Unfortunately, however, it is obvious that the effective exercise of this respect is currently encountering many difficulties.

'Specifically, a state should guard against the creation of new forms of discrimination such as, for example, in the search for accommodation or employment. Public measures in this terrain are often commendably complemented with generous initiatives by associations of volunteers, religious organisations and people of good will who attempt to reduce tension and foster greater social justice by helping their brothers and sisters find employment and decent housing.

'Delicate problems arise when a minority group presents specific claims involving particular political implications. Sometimes a group will seek independence or, at least, greater political autonomy.

'I wish to reiterate that in these delicate situations dialogue and negotiation are the obligatory road to achieving peace. The readiness of the parties to accept one another and initiate dialogue is an indispensable requirement for reaching a fair resolution of complex problems that could seriously jeopardise peace. Otherwise by rejecting dialogue the door can open to violence.

'In certain situations of conflict, terrorist groups unjustly assume the exclusive right of speaking for minority communities, thereby depriving them of a chance to freely and openly elect their own representatives and search, without being intimidated, for the right solutions. Furthermore, the members of these communities suffer only too often from the abusive violence perpetrated in their name.

'Beware those who have chosen the inhuman path of terrorism. Indiscriminate attacks, the killing of innocent people and bloody retaliation does not favour a fair appraisal of the demands made by those minorities in whose name these acts are supposed to be carried out.' (Cf. *Sollicitudo Rei Socialis*, 24).

Duties of Minorities:

'All rights entail their corresponding duties. Members of minority groups also have their own duties to the society and state in which they live.'

a) *The duty to co-operate for the common good*: 'In the first place, they have a duty to co-operate, the same as every other citizen, for the common good. Minorities must, in fact, make their particular contribution towards building a peaceful world that reflects the rich diversity of all its inhabitants.'

b) *The duty to promote the freedom and dignity of each member*: 'In second place, the minority group has a duty to promote the freedom and dignity of each one of its members and respect the decisions of each individual, even when one of them decides to go over to the majority culture.'

c) *The duty to claim respect for legitimate rights*: 'In situations of clear injustice, minority groups of immigrants from abroad have the right to claim respect for the legitimate rights of its members who remain oppressed in their countries of origin and are incapable of making their voices heard. However, considerable wisdom and clear judgement needs to be employed in these cases, especially when there is a lack of objective information as to the living conditions of the affected populations.'

d) *The duty to appraise the bases for one's demands*: 'All members of minority groups, wherever they live, must be able to conscientiously appraise the bases for their demands in the light of historical developments and modern-day realities. Not doing so would incur the risk of remaining prisoners to the past and having no prospects for the future.'

The text ends with an appeal to build peace.

If this doctrine is valid for minorities, then there is all the more reason for it to be valid for nations that do not have a state: the subject of this book. I believe the relationship is evident.

Messages given by Pope John Paul II during his visit to Estonia (10 September 1993)

On 10 September, 1993, John Paul II addressed the men of arts and science of Estonia on the subject of language as the forge of a nation's unity. After reminding his audience of the changes and suffering endured by Estonians under the occupying regime, he said the following:

'2. The long years of dictatorship have managed to torment but not suffocate your national identity. A nation lives on values and traditions so deeply rooted in the soul of its people that they are able to resist even political oppression. This resistance in Estonia has been aided to a large extent by the work of intellectuals who, at the beginning of this century when freedom was first recuperated, devoted themselves to studying the Estonian language carefully, and there found the traditions, culture, the historical memory of your people reflected in their own right. In effect, language is the place where the sedimentation collects, preserving, like a secular repository, the rich and varied cultural heritage of the nation (...)

'There is little doubt that this profound study of Estonian culture should be looked on as far from secondary in developing your national consciousness. In fact language is the vehicle of the experience and civil conquests of a people. In a certain sense it manifests its spirit, bears the mark of its character, of its feelings, its battles and its hopes. The same complex framework reveals dialectal formulations that often document the strain of coexistence and dialogue and the efforts made to unite differences within a common cultural horizon and forge the unity of a nation.'

'3. (...) The historical/philological approach, which tends to value the peculiarities of a specific language, and the structural approach, which, when not driven to radical ideological extremes, tends to demonstrate the contexts and constants of the linguistic phenomenon, offer two complementary approaches that illustrate the many semantic possibilities of language, whether as an instrument of identification, or as a vehicle of communication: both fundamental values that need to be fostered in a balanced synthesis.

'Today, my dear friends, Estonia can finally be itself again. It turns again to its language, its character, its institutions. But it turns to them on an international stage marked by great tensions, where it becomes more necessary than ever to protect a sense of freedom and identity by opening up to dialogue and solidarity. It is up to the intellectuals to perform the delicate task of encouraging this essential synthesis. It means fostering what distinguishes human beings from each other, without forgetting what unites us. In particular, language should be an instrument of identity, and not a separating barrier. This is even more true within a pluri-ethnic context, where respect for the languages and cultures of various social groups is an essential precondition for orderly, peaceful cohabitation.

'The history and culture of our times seem to converge in urging us to speak our own tongues, while building bridges to others' tongues and, above all, making us conscientious listeners and readers of the great language of the universe that unites peoples in the continual, tireless toil of deciphering its mystery.

'4. Therefore, freedom and solidarity, identity and dialogue. The Catholic Church, together with other Christians of various denominations also present in your territory, seek to bear witness to these major, inseparable values (...)'

The Pope continues his discourse and speaks of genuine liberty, the fundamental structure of service to mankind, the urgent need for dialogue and universal joint responsibility.

The above speech was corroborated and complemented by his words that same day – 10 September 1993 – at the end of his pastoral visit to Estonia. They speak of the rights of the individual and the rights of peoples. This highly expressive pairing of the two is frequently used by John Paul II. We see it in the following fragment which captures and underlines it.

'Looking from this point in Europe at the context of European countries, both east and west, from the Atlantic to the Urals, we must again endorse these fundamental rights which allow individuals, communities and peoples to live in peace and mutual respect for each other's rights. The rights of the human being are the foundation of human, Christian, democratic and European civilisation as, too, are the rights of peoples. The words of today's liturgy seem highly appropriate, words considered and meditated upon in the homily. We have to accept one another because Christ has accepted us. We should accept each other in our personal relations. These relationships, in a certain sense, come down to respect for the rights of the human being. Reciprocal acceptance in relations between peoples and states is also expressed through mutual respect of rights between these peoples and these states. The entire order of human coexistence, therefore, is reduced to two sets of rights: the rights of the individual and the rights of peoples.

'Accepting one another means respecting the rights of others between diverse peoples. Large and small countries should enjoy equal respect for their rights. If this reciprocal respect is lacking, we run the risk of going back to what we left behind, because our century has demonstrated how the rights of the individual and peoples can be trampled upon.

'If we are to enter a new Europe that is just, worthy of its tradition and its Christian roots, we need to profoundly reconsider these two orders: the rights of the individual and the rights of peoples.'

The speech continues by insisting that we must replace the old age of fear for an age of 'respect for one another, large and small. All have to be respected. The smallest amongst us in particular have a greater need for their sovereign rights to be respected'. He ends his speech by expressing his gratitude and exhorting his audience to prayer.

Speech given by Pope John Paul II to the Fiftieth General Assembly of the United Nations (New York, 5 October 1995)[2]

Introduction: Greetings, Acknowledgements and Presentation of the Subject

Mr President, distinguished ladies and gentlemen, it is an honour to address this Assembly of peoples, and join the men and women of all countries, races, languages and cultures, in celebrating the fiftieth anniversary of the founding of the United Nations Organisation. I am fully conscious that, in a certain sense, by speaking to this respectable Assembly, I have the opportunity to address the entire family of peoples on the face of the earth. My words, which are meant as a sign of the esteem and interest held by the Apostolic See and the Catholic Church for this Institution, readily join with the voices of those who see in the United Nations Organisation the hope of a better future for the society of men.

In first place, I wish to express my deep gratitude, to the Secretary General, Doctor Boutros Ghali, for warmly encouraging my visit. I am also grateful to you, Mr President, for the cordial welcome I have received from this eminent meeting. I also wish to greet you all and express my acknowledgement of your presence and kind attention.

I have come before you today, with the desire to offer my contribution to the meaningful meditation on the history and

---

[2]This document is presented: a) in its entirety due to its importance; and b) accompanied by detailed subheadings to help the reader better understand its message. These subheadings are different from those in the original text, which are much more brief. Below I list the order of headings as published by *L'Osservatore Romano*, on 6 October 1995:

Introduction (no. 1)
a) A Common Heritage of Humanity (nos. 2–3)
b) Assuming the Risk of Freedom (no. 4)
c) The Rights of Nations (nos. 5–8)
d) The Respect of Differences (nos. 9–11)
e) Freedom and Moral Truth (nos. 12–13)
f) The United Nations and the Future of Freedom (nos. 14–15)
g) Beyond Fear: The Civilisation of Love (nos. 16–18)

role of this Organisation which accompanies and enhances this anniversary. The Holy See, by virtue of the specifically spiritual mission which drives it to diligently seek the integral good of every human being, has resolutely supported the ideals and objectives of the United Nations Organisation since the beginning. Our purpose and mode of operation are obviously different, but the common concern for the human family continually opens up vast areas for the Church and the UN to co-operate.

It is this conviction which guides and inspires my reflections today. They will not dwell on specific social, political or economic questions, rather on the extraordinary changes that have occurred in recent years and their consequences for the present and future of all humanity.

1. The Universal Quest for Freedom Involves Individuals and Nations

The Individual [A) and B)]

The universal quest for freedom, based on human rights, gathers pace

The universal quest for freedom gathers pace

Ladies and gentlemen, at the dawn of a new millennium we are witnessing an extraordinary, world-wide accelerated quest for freedom which is one of the great driving forces of the history of mankind. This phenomenon is not limited to a single part of the world, nor is it the expression of a single culture. On the contrary, men and women in every corner of the earth, even though threatened by violence, have faced the risk of freedom to ask to be given the recognition in social, political and economic life that their dignity as free individuals deserves. This universal quest for freedom is truly one of the distinguishing features of our times.

The universal quest for freedom is based on the rights of man

On 2 October 1979, during my previous visit to the United Nations, I had the opportunity to highlight how the quest for freedom in our times is based on the universal rights which man enjoys due to the simple fact of being one. It was precisely the outrages committed against human dignity which led the United Nations Organisation to draw up, barely three years after its constitution, the Universal Declaration of Human Rights, which continues to be one of the highest expressions of the human conscience in our time. In Asia and Africa, in the Americas, in Oceania and in Europe, courageous, decided men and women have appealed to this Declaration to strengthen their claims for greater participation in the life of society.

The inner structure of this world movement

Characteristics

Universality   It is important for us to understand what we could call the inner structure of this world movement. A first and fundamental 'key' is precisely offered by its planetary character, confirming that there indeed do exist universal human rights rooted in the nature of the individual which reflect the essential, objective demands of a universal moral law. Far from being abstract statements, these rights tell us something rather important about the individual life of every man and every social group.

Moral logic   They also remind us that we do not live in an irrational, meaningless world but, on the contrary, there is a moral logic that illuminates human existence and makes dialogue between men and peoples possible. If we want a century of constraint to give way to a century of persuasion, we need to find a way to discuss the future of man using an understandable, common language. Universal moral law, engraved in the hearts of men, is a form of 'grammar' that helps the world face this discussion of its future.

Objection and reply

Objection   In this sense, the fact that some may today deny the universality of human rights, just as they deny there is a human nature common to all, is a serious concern.

Reply Certainly, there is no single model for organising the politics and economics of human freedom, as different cultures and diverse historical experiences lead a free, responsible society to different institutional forms. However, it is one thing to assert the legitimate pluralism of the 'forms of freedom' and another to deny the universal or intelligible character of the nature of man or the human experience. The latter makes an international policy of persuasion very difficult or even impossible.

Historical proof: the non-violent revolutions of 1989

Personal perspective

The moral impetuses of the universal quest for freedom clearly appeared in Central and Eastern Europe with the non-violent revolutions of 1989. Those events, occurring in specific times and places, have nevertheless offered a lesson that goes beyond the geographical confines of a specific place. The non-violent revolutions of 1989 have demonstrated that the quest for freedom is an inevitable demand that arises from the recognition of the inestimable value and dignity of the human being, and is always accompanied by a commitment to his advance. Above all, modern totalitarianism has been an assault on the dignity of the individual, an assault that has even gone to the point of negating the inviolable value of his life. The revolutions of 1989 have been made possible by the effort of courageous men and women inspired by a different, and ultimately, more profound and vigorous vision: the vision of man as an intelligent, free individual, repository of a transcending mystery, endowed with the capacity to reflect and choose, and, therefore, capable of wisdom and virtue.

The perspective of solidarity

A decisive factor for the success of these non-violent revolutions was the experience of social solidarity: in the face of regimes backed by the force of propaganda and terror, solidarity formed the moral nucleus of the 'power of the powerless', it was a beacon of hope and continues to be a reminder of the means available to man to continue, in his way through history, along the path of the noblest aspirations of the human spirit.

Common ground: values and the United Nations charter

Looking back today on those events from this privileged world observatory, it is impossible not to see the common ground uniting the values which inspired those people's liberation movements and many of the moral obligations laid down in the United Nations Charter. I am reminded, for example, of the duty to 'reassert faith in the fundamental rights of man, in the dignity and value of the human being'; and also the duty to 'promote social progress and raise living standards within a wider concept of freedom' (preamble). The fifty-one states who founded this Organisation in 1945 truly lit a torch whose light is capable of dispersing the darkness of tyranny, a light which can show the path of freedom, of peace and solidarity.

The nations [C), D) and E)]

Contemporary events which demonstrate the quest for freedom undertaken by nations

The quest for freedom seen in the second half of the twentieth century has not only involved individuals but nations as well.

Violations of the freedom of nations

The Second World War   Fifty years after the end of the Second World War it is important to remember that the conflict originated with the violation of the rights of nations. Many of those nations suffered tremendously for no other reason than for being considered 'other'. Terrible crimes were committed in the name of awful doctrines which preached the 'inferiority' of certain nations and cultures. In a certain sense, it may be said that the United Nations Organisation was born of the conviction that these doctrines were incompatible with peace; and the Charter's efforts to 'save future generations from the scourge of war' (preamble) surely implied the moral commitment to defend every nation and culture from unjust, violent aggression.

The post-war period   Unfortunately, even after the end of the Second World War the rights of nations continued to be violated. To give only a few examples, the Baltic States and large areas of the Ukraine and Byelorussia were absorbed by the Soviet Union, as had occurred with Armenia, Azerbaijan and Georgia in the Caucasus. At the same time, the so-called 'People's Democracies' of Central and Eastern Europe in effect lost their sovereignty and were required to submit to the will dominating the entire block. The result of this artificial division of Europe was the 'Cold War', that is to say, a situation of international tension where the threat of nuclear holocaust hung over humanity.

The restoration of the freedom of nations

It was only when freedom was restored to the nations of Central and Eastern Europe, that the promise of peace which should have arrived with the end of the war began to be realised for many victims of that conflict.

Global historical perspective: yesterday and today in the question of the right of nations

Comment

The Universal Declaration of the Rights of Man, adopted in 1948, eloquently dealt with the rights of the individual, but there is still no similar international agreement that adequately addresses the rights of nations. This is a situation that needs to be carefully considered, as it raises urgent questions about justice and freedom in the contemporary world.

The problem of the recognition of the rights of nations recurs

Yesterday: the Council of Constance, the University of Salamanca, Benedict XV In fact, the consciousness of humanity has been repeatedly presented with the problem of the full recognition of the rights of peoples and nations, giving rise to considerable ethical-juridical reflection. I am reminded of the debate developed during the Council of Constance in the fifteenth century, when the representatives of the Academy of Krakow, led by Pawel Wlodkowic, tenaciously defended the right of certain European populations to existence and autonomy. Around the same time, the reflections regarding the peoples of the New World which went on at the University of

Salamanca, are very well known. Furthermore, in this century, how can we forget the prophetic words of my predecessor Benedict XV who, during the First World War reminded us all that 'nations do not die', and invited us to 'consider with a calm conscience the rights and just hopes of peoples?' (*To the Peoples at War and their Leaders*, 28 July 1915.)

Today: the problem of nationalities forms part of a new, particular world horizon – an anthropological reflection

Today, the problem of nationalities forms part of a new world horizon characterised by large-scale 'mobility' which makes the selfsame ethno-cultural confines of different peoples ever less well defined, because of various processes such as migration, the mass media and the globalisation of the economy. However, it is precisely against this horizon of universality that we see the pressing action of ethno-cultural particularities surging up as some impulsive need for identity and survival, a kind of counter-weight to the tendency to uniformity. It is something we should not underestimate, as if it were some simple residue of the past. It needs serious examination, and deep anthropological, ethical and juridical reflection.

'Particular-universal' tension, inherent to the human being

We can consider this tension between the particular and the universal as being inherent to the human being. Their common nature makes men feel they are part of a single large family, as is the case. However, because of the specific history of this nature, they will be more strongly tied to certain human groups; first of all the family, followed by various peer groups, reaching all the way down to their respective ethno-cultural group which, by no accident, employs the term 'nation' evoking the word 'natal', while the term 'patria' (father or mother land) evokes the family itself. The human condition is therefore located between these two poles – universality and particularity – that are in continual tension; inevitable tension, but one that is especially fruitful when lived in calm equilibrium.

The rights of nations rest on this anthropological foundation

The 'Rights of Nations' also rest upon this anthropological foundation, after all, they are no other than 'human rights' experienced at the specific level of community life.

This anthropological reflection, though not easy, is important
The reflection of these rights is certainly not easy, bearing in mind the difficulty of defining the concept of 'nation', which cannot be identified *a priori* or necessarily with state. However, it is an important subject worthy of reflection if we wish to avoid the errors of the past and ensure a just world order.

Ethical and Juridical Reflection

Specific listing of some rights of nations (the expression of particularity)

1) *The right to exist*

An absolute premise for the other rights of a nation is its right to exist: no one then – whether state, another nation or international organisation – can legitimately believe that a nation has no right to exist. This fundamental right to exist does not necessarily require state sovereignty, as there are several possible forms of juridical aggregation as occurs, for example, in Federal States, Confederations or states characterised by wide-ranging regional autonomies. There may be historical circumstances where aggregations distinct from a sovereign sate can even prove advisable, but with the condition that this occurs in a climate of true freedom, guaranteed by the exercise of self-determination by the peoples.

2) *The right to one's own language*

The right to exist naturally enough implies that each nation also has the right to its own language and culture, through which a people expresses and promotes what I would call its original spiritual 'sovereignty'. History shows us that in extreme circumstances (such as those seen in the land where I was born), it is precisely its culture which enables a nation to survive the loss of its political and economic independence.

3) *The right to shape one's life according to one's traditions*

All nations also consequently have the right to shape their lives according to their traditions, except, of course, all violation of fundamental human rights and, in particular, the oppression of minorities.

4) *The right to build one's own future*

Every nation has the right to build its own future, by providing the younger generations a suitable education.

Regarding the rights of nations (the expression of universality)
If the 'rights of the nation' express the vital requirements of 'particularity', it is no less important to stress the requirements of 'universality', expressed though a clear awareness of the duties that nations have to one another and humanity as a whole. Certainly, the first of these is the duty to live in an attitude of peace, respect and solidarity with other nations.

Synthesis: the balanced exercise of rights and duties   By the exercise of the rights of nations, balanced by the assertion and practice of duties, a fruitful 'exchange of talents' is thereby promoted, which in turn reinforces unity among men.

Respect for differences

Over the past seventeen years, during my pastoral pilgrimages to the communities of the Catholic Church, I have been able to enter into dialogue with the rich diversity of nations and cultures in every part of the world.

The world has yet to learn to live with diversity
Unfortunately, the world has yet to learn to live with diversity, as the recent events in the Balkans and Central Africa have painfully reminded us. The reality of the 'difference' and peculiarity of 'the other' can sometimes feel like a weight, or even a threat. The fear of 'difference' fed by historical resentments and exacerbated by the manipulations of the unscrupulous, can lead to the denial of the 'other's' humanity, with the result that people fall into a spiral of violence where no one is spared, not even children. We are all well aware of these situations, and the suffering of the martyred populations of Bosnia-Herzegovina is especially present in my heart and my prayers at this moment.

From bitter experience, then, we all know that fear of 'differences', especially when expressed by a narrow, exclusive nationalism that denies any rights to the 'other', can lead to a true nightmare of violence and terror.

There is a fundamental communion beyond our differences
Yet, if we make an effort to look at things objectively, we can see that beyond all the differences that characterise individuals and peoples, there lies a fundamental commonalty, as the different

cultures in reality are but diverse ways of dealing with the meaning of personal existence. Precisely here we can identify a source of the respect due to every culture and every nation: all cultures are an effort of reflection on the mystery of the world and, in particular, man. It is a way of expressing the transcendent dimension of human life. The heart of every culture is formed by its approach to the greatest of all mysteries: the mystery of God.

Therefore, our respect for the cultures of others is based on our respect for the effort made by each community to answer the question of human life. In this context, we can see the importance of safeguarding the fundamental right to freedom of religion and freedom of belief as essential pillars for the structure of human rights and the foundation of all truly free societies. No one is permitted to violate these rights by using coercive power to impose an answer to the mystery of man.

Regret for diversity or attempting to annul it is cutting oneself off from the depths of the mystery of human life

To want to ignore the reality of diversity – or worse yet, trying to annul it – means to exclude the chance of sounding the depths of the mystery of human life. The truth about man is the unchangeable criteria by which all cultures are judged, but every culture has something to teach about one or other dimension of that complex truth. Therefore, the 'difference' which some find so threatening, through respectful dialogue, can become a source of deep understanding on the mystery of human existence.

Two essentially different types of nationalism

In this context it is necessary to clarify the essential difference between a dangerous form of nationalism, which preaches contempt for other nations or cultures, and patriotism which, in contrast, is just love for one's own country.

Patriotism (nationalism that loves its own country)   True patriotism never attempts to promote the interests of its own country at the expense of others. In the end, this brings harm to one's nation too, producing destructive effects to both the aggressor and the victim.

Exacerbated nationalism   Nationalism, especially in its more radical expressions, is therefore opposed to true patriotism, and today we must ensure that exacerbated nationalism does not continue to propose new aberrations of totalitarianism. Obviously, this commitment also holds true even when the religious principle is assumed as the foundation for nationalism, as sadly occurs in certain manifestations of so-called 'fundamentalism'.

Living in freedom is a great challenge for the vitality of nations

The fundamental question is the responsible use of freedom

Ladies and gentlemen, freedom is the measure of man's dignity and greatness. Living in the freedom that individuals and peoples seek is a great challenge for the spiritual growth of mankind and the moral vitality of nations. The fundamental question, which we today all need to face, is the responsible use of freedom, both in its personal and social dimension. It is therefore necessary for our reflection to turn on the question of the moral structure of freedom: the inner architecture of the culture of freedom.

Freedom has a moral structure which is the inner architecture of the culture of freedom

Freedom has an inner logic; it is ordered to the truth, it is lived in the quest for and in acting in truth   Freedom is not the simple absence of tyranny or oppression, nor is it a licence to do as you please. Freedom possesses an inner 'logic' which distinguishes and ennobles it: it is ordered to truth and is lived in the quest for and fulfilment of truth.

Detached from truth, freedom degenerates into licentiousness (individual life) and arbitrariness (political life)   Detached from the truth of the individual, freedom decays in individual life into licentiousness and in political life into the arbitrariness of the fittest and the arrogance of power.

Reference to the truth about man is the guarantee for the future of freedom   Therefore, far from being a limitation or a threat to freedom, reference to the truth about mankind, universally recognised truth because of the moral law inscribed in everyone's heart, is, in fact, the guarantee for the future of freedom.

Comparison with utilitarianism

As the advantageous is sought instead of the good, utilitarianism threatens freedom and hinders the culture of freedom

In the light of what has been said we can see how utilitarianism, a doctrine which defines morality not on the basis of what is good but on the basis of what is most advantageous, is a threat to individual and national freedom, and hinders the construction of a true culture of freedom.

Politically, it inspires an aggressive nationalism   Utilitarianism often has negative political consequences because it inspires an aggressive nationalism, on the basis of which subjugating a smaller or weaker nation is considered good, simply because it responds to national interests.

Economically, it drives stronger countries to exploiting and manipulating the weaker ones   No less serious are the consequences of economic utilitarianism, which leads stronger countries to manipulating and taking advantage of weaker ones.

In the same vein, both forms characterise north–south relations   Frequently these two forms of utilitarianism go hand in hand, and is a phenomenon which has notoriously characterised relations between the 'North' and the 'South'. For developing nations, attaining political independence has often brought with it economic dependence on other countries. It should be emphasised that in some cases developing areas have even suffered such a backward slide that some states lack the means to answer the basic needs of their peoples.

These situations pose a formidable challenge for the human family

Insult and challenge   These situations insult humanity's conscience and pose a formidable moral challenge to the human family.

Meeting the challenge requires changes from developed and under-developed countries

Meeting this challenge obviously requires changes both in developing countries and in the economically most advanced. If the former can offer firm guarantees for the proper management of resources and aid, as well as respect for human rights and, if necessary, replacing unjust, corrupt or authoritarian forms of government with participatory, democratic ones, would this not open the way to better civil and economic resources for the people themselves? While, for their part, should not developed countries perhaps be more mature and renounce strictly utilitarian approaches to adopt an approach characterised by greater justice and solidarity?

It is important to prescribe an ethic of solidarity   Surely, illustrious ladies and gentlemen, it is necessary to prescribe an ethic of solidarity on the international economic scene, if we want participation, economic growth and a just distribution of goods to characterise the future of humanity. International co-operation, under the auspices of the United Nations Charter 'to solve international problems of an economic, social, cultural and humanitarian nature', (art. 1, 3), cannot be exclusively conceived in terms of aid or assistance, or even by considering the eventual return on resources made available. When millions suffer poverty – meaning hunger, malnutrition, disease, illiteracy and misery – not only should we remember that no one has the right to exploit another for his own benefit, but also, and above all, the need to reaffirm our commitment to solidarity, which enables others to live in specific economic and political circumstances; our commitment to creativity, a characteristic of the human being which makes the wealth of nations possible.

2. In the Face of Current Challenges, the UN plays an Increasingly Necessary Role [F)]

[F)]

From administrative institution to the moral centre, where nations feel at home

In the face of these enormous challenges, how can we fail to acknowledge the role of the United Nations Organisation? Fifty years after its inception, the need for such an Organisation seems even more obvious: however, based on experience, it is also clearer to see that the effectiveness of this great instrument for the synthesis and co-ordination of international life depends on the international culture and ethics on which it is based and expresses. The United Nations Organisation needs to rise even more above the cold condition of an administrative institution and be the moral centre, where all the world's nations feel at home, developing a common sense of being, as it were, a 'family of nations'.

The characteristics of the family

The concept of 'family' immediately evokes something which goes beyond simple functional relations or a mere convergence of interests. By its nature, the family is a community based on reciprocal trust, mutual help and sincere respect. In a real family there is no domination by the strong: on the contrary, it is precisely because of their weakness that the weak are all the more welcomed and helped.

Treating the UNO as a 'Family of Nations'

Transferred to the 'family of nations', these are the sentiments that relations between peoples need to create, even before the law itself.

From the organisational to the organic level, from co-existence to pro-existence

The UNO has the historical, if not epic, mission to favour this qualitative leap in international life, not only as a centre of effective mediation for the resolution of conflicts, but also by promoting attitudes, values and specific initiatives of solidarity which are capable of raising relations between nations from the 'organisational' level to the, as it were, 'organic' level; from the simple 'existence with' others to the 'existence for' others, in a fruitful exchange of talents which is especially advantageous for the weaker nations, but also clearly favours the well-being of all.

This is the way to achieve the participation of peoples, in full esteem for every cultural identity

Only under this condition will we surpass not just the 'wars of combat', but also the 'cold wars'; not just the equality of rights between all peoples, but also their active participation in the construction of a better future; not just respect for every cultural identity, but full esteem for the common wealth of the cultural heritage of humanity. Is this not the ideal proposed by the United Nations Charter when it declares the basis of the Organisation to be 'the principle of the sovereign equality of all its members' (art. 2,1), or when it commits itself to 'fostering relations of friendship between nations based on respect for the principle of equality of rights and the free determination of peoples' (art. 1,2)?

This high-road has to be followed to the end

This is the high-road that should be followed to the end, even if this involves appropriate modifications of the operating model of the United Nations, if necessary, in order to take into account all that has occurred in this half century, with so many new peoples assuming the experience of freedom in the legitimate hope of 'being' and 'counting for' more.

We need to remove the paralysing burden of cynicism

This should not appear to be some unattainable utopia. It is the time for new hope calling on us to remove the paralysing burden of cynicism from the future of the politics and lives of men.

From the risk of freedom to the risks of solidarity and peace

The anniversary we are celebrating invites us to do precisely this, the idea of the 'united nations' anew proposing a concept that speaks eloquently of mutual trust, security and solidarity. Inspired by the example of those who have assumed the risk of freedom, could we not also take on the risk of solidarity, and therefore the risk of peace?

3. We Must All Build the Civilisation of Love Together in Response to Our Fear of the Future [G)]

[G)]

A paradox: modern man (from maturity to independence) comes to the end of the twentieth century in fear of himself, his works and the future

One of the greatest paradoxes of our time is that man, who began the period we call 'modernity' with the self-confident affirmation of his 'maturity' and 'independence', comes to the end of the twentieth century fearful of himself, frightened by what he is capable of, and afraid of the future. In fact, the second half of the twentieth century has seen the unprecedented phenomenon of a humanity uncertain about the possibility of a future, given the threat of nuclear war. This danger, thank God, seems to have receded – and everything which could make it return needs to be firmly and universally rejected, for fear that it should again rise up – however, the fear for and of the future remains.

We must regain a spirit of trust and hope

In order for the new millennium at our door to witness a new zenith of the human spirit, favoured by an authentic culture of freedom, humanity needs to learn to overcome its fear. We must learn to not be afraid and regain a spirit of hope and trust. Hope is no vain optimism dictated by the naive trust that the future will necessarily be better than the past.

Both feed in the last sanctuary of conscience, where they are alone with God

Hope and trust are the premises of a responsible action and receives its support in the intimate sanctuary of conscience where 'man is alone with God' (*Gaudim et spes*, 16), and he therefore senses that he is not alone among the enigmas of existence, because the love of the Creator accompanies him!

They involve the recovery of the transcendental horizon to which the human spirit journeys

Hope and trust may seem to be subjects beyond the remit of the United Nations. In fact this is not so, because the political actions of nations, the main concern of your Organisation, always involve the transcendental, spiritual dimension of human experience, and cannot be ignored without harming the cause of mankind and human freedom. All that diminishes man harms the cause of freedom. In order to regain our hope and trust at the end of this century of suffering, we must regain sight of the transcendental horizon of possibilities to which the human spirit journeys.

One man's testimony: my hope and trust are based on Jesus Christ, God made man

Furthermore, as a Christian, it is impossible for me to not bear witness that my hope and trust are based on Jesus Christ, the two thousandth anniversary of whose birth will be celebrated at the dawn of the new millennium. We Christians believe that His Death and Resurrection fully revealed the love of God and His concern for all creation. For us, Jesus Christ is God made man, and has entered the history of humanity.

Christian hope extends to every human being

Precisely for this reason, the Christian hope for the world and its future extends to every human being. There is nothing truly human that does not resonate in the hearts of Christians.

Faith in Christ obliges us to conduct a respectful dialogue with other men

Faith in Christ does not drive us to intolerance, on the contrary, it obliges us to maintain a respectful dialogue with other men.

Love for Christ asks us to show concern for others

Love for Christ does not stop us from being interested in others, rather it asks us to show concern for them, to the exclusion of no one and, if anything, granting a privileged place to those who are weaker and are suffering. Therefore, as we approach the second millennium of Christ's birth, the Church only asks to be respectfully allowed to propose this message of salvation and to promote solidarity for the entire human family, in the spirit of charity and service.

I stand here as a witness

Ladies and gentlemen, I stand here before you, as my predecessor Pope Paul VI did exactly thirty years ago, not as one who exercises temporal power – in his words – nor as a religious leader invoking special privileges for his community. I stand here before you as a witness:

- a witness to the dignity of man,
- a witness to hope,
- a witness to the conviction that the destiny of each nation is in the hands of compassionate Providence.

A goal: we must build the civilisation of love in response to our fear for the future

We must vanquish our fear of the future. However, we cannot vanquish it completely unless we do so together. The 'response' to this fear is not coercion, or repression or the imposition of a single social 'model' on the entire world. The response to the fear that blinds human existence at the end of the century is the common effort to build the civilisation of love, based on the universal values of peace, of solidarity, of justice and freedom.

The soul of the civilisation of love is the culture of individual and national freedom

And the 'soul' of the civilisation of love is the culture of freedom: the freedom of individuals and the freedom of nations, lived in self-giving solidarity and responsibility.

Every individual has been created in the image and likeness of God

We should not be afraid of the future. We should not be afraid of man. We do not find ourselves here by chance. Each person has been created in the 'image and likeness' of the One who is the origin of all that exists.

With wisdom, virtue and the grace of God

We have within us the capacity for wisdom and virtue. With these two gifts, and the help of God's grace, we can build the century that is upon us and the next millennium:

- a civilisation worthy of the human being,
- a true culture of freedom.

Conclusion

We can and should do so! And, by doing so, we will see that the tears of this century have prepared the ground for a new springtime of the human spirit.

'The Christian Roots of Catalonia', by the Bishops of Catalonia (27 December 1985)[3]

Ten centuries ago now, Catalonia, a political entity born from the rump of Carolingian Europe and formed out of the Spanish March, removed itself from beneath all trans-Pyrenean subjugation and embarked upon its own path through history.

Today, one thousand years later, our people are again experiencing a new situation. The restoration of political autonomy, implemented by the Spanish Constitution of 1978 and made reality by the Statute of 1979, have created a new situation which the years are consolidating. The acknowledgement of a specific Catalan culture, expressed especially through its language, is combined with the recognition of its nationality and the right to self-government. This has consequences on the lives of its citizens, from the contents of the subjects taught at the various levels of education to a multitude of aspects in administrative and political life. It may be said that autonomy gives a sense of self-possession to democratic life in our country.

The majority of Christians in our dioceses, together with other citizens, unquestionably share a feeling of satisfaction for this advance in freedom. Many have even been courageous, energetic instigators of this advance through some difficult years.

Nevertheless, there are those who feel somewhat perplexed, a situation which may be explained by the variety of information put across by various social groups and different regions, by the relative speed with which changes have occurred, and the significant presence of brothers from other nations and regions in our communities, as well as the memory of certain facets of our recent history and the image adopted by Catholicism during that period.

Therefore, to the list of important subjects offered by the Episcopal Conference of Tarragona for reflection by our faithful congregation, we now wish to add a few simple thoughts on the reality of Catalonia. In the first place, they are offered to the Christians of our dioceses in order to provide clear-cut points of

---

[3]Published by Altés, S. L., Barcelona 1986. I believe that the inclusion of this document, in its entirety and the collective labour of the bishops of Catalonia, notably enhances this book.

reference, and to all our people as a means for our episcopal ministry to contribute to the common good of the country.

Furthermore, Catalonia quite clearly falls within the scope of the contribution made by Christianity to European culture, a view expressed by John Paul II in his speech to UNESCO on 2 June 1980: 'It would be no exaggeration to state that, through a multitude of events, across the history of each nation and every community, the whole of Europe – from the Atlantic to the Urals – bears witness to the link that exists between culture and Christianity.'

Love and service to Catalonia

There are words that due to certain circumstances are discredited. One of these is the term 'patriotism', which is hardly ever used today. Even when referring to a country, words such as 'love' and 'esteem' are rarely used in certain highly critical, rationalist, contemporary media. In his time, Pius XII protested about 'this fear which citizens these days sometimes have of appearing to be generously inclined to their own country'.[4]

The cause of this lies in the ambivalence often stirred by these words, in the self-motivated, hypocritical use that some may have made of them, or the exaggerations and extreme views which some may attempt to justify by these concepts.

In the case of love for Catalonia, we also find other negative factors: poor historical and political education given at school, and the confusion it creates; lack of knowledge on Catalan identity; the impression this identity gives some people of division, extremism or even something to be suspicious of from the religious standpoint.

However, whatever the term employed, it is fundamental for us to begin by referring to love for Catalonia as forming part of love for one's fellow man. It consists of the our basic solidarity for those around us, not simply in the individual sense, but also as part of our social reality: the family, our country, our social class, etc.

Although sometimes it may not be due to egoism in the strict sense of the word, it is true that we do not necessarily demonstrate the appropriate respect. This may occur because of the

---

[4]Allocution to the Colony of Marches, Rome, 23 March 1958.

lack of good information and a moral education based on indi-
vidualism hinders us from seeing the individual in the broad
context of his relationships. We need to correct these deficien-
cies in order to prevent the types of scandals sometimes
produced by believers who, despite invoking charity in matters
regarding individual needs and concern for anecdotal cases, lack
compassion when it comes to large-scale collective aspirations
and the task of promoting the social groups to which they
belong.

Insofar as the concept under consideration, we wish to show
the reader that Catalonia forms the basic community and
cultural unit for all its citizens and, therefore, its point of entry
into universal culture. 'Between the family and universal
culture, one's country forms part of the order desired by God,'
declared Cardinal Feltin.[5]

It would be a mistake to think that references to real life or,
very often, to simple, generalised concepts could replace
prompt compassion, or even that it is enough. A false, universally held belief abounds which is impractical and even serves as
an excuse for certain selfish interests. Certainly our love knows
no limits and in no way ends with our country. But it is equally
true that it needs to pass through it and is forged by it.

Obviously, this love involves a commitment to civic-minded-
ness that becomes manifest in the fulfilment of one's social
duties. In effect, every citizen – and it is important for us Christians to expect more from ourselves – has to accept just laws,
and not escape from them arbitrarily in an attempt for more
advantageous conditions. As the Second Vatican Council
taught, 'the duty of justice and charity is increasingly met by
the fact that each one of us, by contributing to the common
good according to our own abilities and the needs of others, also
promotes and favours the public and private institutions that
help transform and improve the living conditions of men'. It
continues, 'there are those who, though professing open-
minded, generous opinions, in fact always live as if they are not
in the least concerned about society. What is more, many, in
various places, pay no heed to the laws and mores of society.
More than a few, by means of fraud and cheating, show no

---

[5]*La conciencia cristiana y los nacionalismos* (Christian Conscience and Nationalism), French Catholic intellectual week, Barcelona, 1966, p. 14.

remorse about evading their fair contributions and other rights they owe society'.[6] With the result that when social morals deteriorate at some or other point, there is always someone that suffers the consequences.

The responsibility and duty to foster the common good more closely affects those who, by vocation or ability, are involved in government or policy due to public office. It is important that they always maintain a sense of service for the common good that is greater than their personal or group interests. They have to remember that all resources – parties, programmes, elections, governments, parliaments, town councils, etc. – are at the service of the common good, and not the other way round.

For the Christian, this commitment has a further dimension. It is the vehicle through which the Gospel is made present and permeates the world with influence.

Currently we are all noticing a certain decline in Christian values in the general public, but rather than succumbing to regret and accusation, we should examine if we are being generous and creative enough to achieve an active presence that communicates our faith throughout the social, cultural and institutional fabric of Catalan society. In the same vein, we have to note that refusing to serve one's country to the best of one's abilities constitutes a sin of omission. The allergy to political activity entails leaving community interests exclusively to others.

As for the political action of Christians, needless to say it should always be exemplary. It should clearly show the spirit of service we have referred to and, as a result of this spirit, a greater desire for coexistence and co-operation with all, even with non-believers when they work from positions that concur with ethics and the common good, and involve special consideration for the unfortunate.

The fact of Catalan nationality

In the press communiqué issued after our meeting on 20 July 1979, we said, 'In the current political climate, as on previous occasions, we, the bishops of Catalonia, declare our desire for the civil legislation on Catalonia that is being drawn up to fully

---

[6]*Gaudium et spes*, no. 30.

recognise the rights of our people to their national identity, demonstrated in the reality of their culture and history.'

We believe that it is also our pastoral duty to help clarify the issue of Catalan national identity, which has raised so much heated and emotional controversy in some circles, frequently because of terminology. In fact, we do not always take into sufficient account the relative or functional efficiency of words in expressing the meaning or content we wish to convey.

In contrast to what has occurred in other places, Catalan culture in historical writing, literature, thought, politics and broad popular sectors has kept alive the distinction between nation and state. Prat de la Riba, who understood the nation to be synonymous with the mother country, expressed this as follows, 'The state is an artificial, voluntary, political body. The mother country is an historical, natural and necessary community. The former is the creation of men, the latter is fruit of the laws to which God has subjected the lives of generations of man.'[7] The venerable Torras i Bages explained that he wrote his book *La tradició catalana* to clarify the question: 'Do our people have a true personal sense of being capable of a life of its own? If the concept of person can be applied to the Catalan people, in other words, if, as the ancient scholars used to say, *indivisum in se et divisum ab aliis* (indivisible in itself and distinct from others), if it is a rational individual with a will and intelligence of its own, nobody can deny it the right to life.'[8] Using a terminology that rings very strange to our modern ears, this towering text helps us understand that in fact we are dealing, not with defending the name of the nation as some label, but the acknowledgement of a factual reality.

As bishops of the Church in Catalonia, embodied in its people, we testify to the national reality of Catalonia reflected over a thousand years of history and we also demand that the doctrine of the Church Magistracy be applied to her: the rights and cultural values of ethnic minorities within a state, of its peoples, nations or nationalities, must be respected absolutely and even championed by the state, who may in no way, in all law and justice, persecute them, destroy them or assimilate them into a majority culture.

The existence of the Catalan nation calls for an appropriate

[7] *Doctrina catalanista* (Catalan Doctrine), Mexico, 1953, p. 29
[8] *La tradició catalana*, 8, from The Complete Works, Barcelona, 1948, pp. 5–6.

legal-political structure which makes the exercise of these rights viable. The most adequate form for specifically recognising nationality, with its concomitant rights and prerogatives, is the direct responsibility of civil regulation.

The widely-spread confusion between nation and state leads to suspicion and mistrust: many interpret the assertion of nationality as a demand for a separate state, something which is, in fact, not a necessary consequence. By employing the right organisational structure, a state can achieve coexistence and progress for the various nations it embraces, without any of them feeling compelled to be assimilated by another.

Peoples who, as in the case of Catalonia, are conscious of their history before the state was formed, and preserve alongside this awareness, a culture and language of their own that do not belong to the majority in the state, are convinced that they are not the result of an administrative division in a nation state, but are a component of a plurinational state with their own personality. This consciousness of having been a national reality before which has joined others to form a state, is what gives our country a sense of nation and means that the autonomy and institutions it has regained are looked on, not as some political fashion, but the answer to deep, irrefutable, historical aspirations.

We would like our Catholic brothers from other peoples in Spain to be the first to recognise and welcome these aspirations. In contrast, we Catalan Catholics would also have to be the first in opening up to their problems. Carles Cardó, in 1930, remarked on the important repercussions for peace in Spain if Catholics were to embark on the noble task of helping their fellow citizens understand problems experienced by others. He proposed conducting a round of self-criticism from the perspective of Catalonia and asked other Spaniards to let go of 'the disastrous idea that confuses organic, unique, living unity with mechanical unity, which is always dead or about to die'. But, as the distinguished thinker stressed, the painful paradox often arises that 'those who do not have the light of faith show this Christian understanding and are ready for the glory, prestige and profit of its application. Many Catholics, in contrast, cling on stubbornly in impenetrable incomprehension'.[9] It is a call to

---

[9] *La nit transparent* (The Transparent Night), published by La Paraula Cristiana, Barcelona, 1935, p. 181.

Catholics to assume responsibility which has not lost its relevance today.

It should be said that, in remembering the need to clarify between the concepts of the nation and the state for the sake of an accurate interpretation of present-day realities, we do not intend to reduce the ties of brotherhood and solidarity between the peoples of Spain to a purely administrative relationship. Our common history, with all that is good in it and all that has been negative, our interrelationships, swelled in our times by migration, our major underlying affinities, in which our shared faith plays an extremely important role, have all woven a solid basis for understanding, affection and co-operation between us all. However, it will only be possible to move forward if the political and administrative forms adopted by the state do not at any time hinder the natural development of each people but, instead, benefit and serve them.

A culture

Pope John Paul II, in his speech to UNESCO, referred to the plurality of cultures: 'Culture is a specific way for man to *exist* and *be*. Man always adheres to a culture of his own, but which in turn makes a commonly held "nexus" between men and which establishes the inter-personal and social nature of man's existence. The *unity* of culture, as a peculiarity of human existence, is further anchored to the *plurality of cultures* in which man lives. Man grows within this plurality without losing his essential contact with the unity of culture as the fundamental, essential dimension of his existence and being.'[10]

On many occasions the firm will of the Catalans to preserve, come what may, their repeatedly threatened culture has been interpreted as unwarranted obstinacy.

However, our people have seen that by abandoning their cultural identity they would lose their 'nexus' with human culture, to describe it in the terms used by the Pope. Universality has never been understood in Catalonia as a reductive process of subordination to a hegemonic culture, but as a reinforcement of each culture and its responsible contribution to the service of mankind. It should be pointed out that history

---

[10]Allocution to UNESCO, 2 June 1980.

confirms this conviction: it was during the zenith of Catalan culture when Catalonia made its greatest contributions to universal culture.

Above all, Catalan culture finds its expression and principal mark of identity – although not the only one – in its own language, which it shares with other sister communities.

This language has known periods of splendour and periods of decline. It has been the official language of chancelleries and the language of exile, but the people have always kept it alive, loved it and defended it.

Today, after a period of marginalisation, it is again the official language and its use in our society is beginning to return to normal, in the hope of recovering lost time and reaching levels of usage appropriate for the language of a country. We, the bishops of Catalonia, are pleased to see this fact and wish to contribute to society's general effort in fully re-establishing the language of Ramon Llull and Jacint Verdaguer. These words by John Paul II to the young people of Tokyo, spoken on 24 February 1981, resound with special force for us: 'The culture of each nation is expressed, among other ways yet more than any other, in language. Language is the form we give to our thoughts, it is like a robe onto which we pin these thoughts. Language embraces the peculiar traits which give a people and a nation their identity. And, in some way, the heart of the nation lies latent within it, because language, one's own language, gives expression to what feeds man's soul in the community of a family, of a nation, of history.'

Insofar as the contribution of the Church to the normal, everyday use of the Catalan language goes, we are pleased to emphasise how important the Catalan version of all liturgical books has been – and the warm reception it has received. The full introduction of Catalan in the Catholic liturgy – accomplished as soon as the Holy See authorised the liturgical use of the vernacular in times that were still difficult for our language – was a historic event which, in addition to the pastoral progress made as a result of more enthusiastic participation by the community in religious celebrations, has further strengthened the language.

A period of change

Culture, all cultures, evolves with man. Catalonia, which over a century ago first saw the typical changes industrial society brings, has since seen its counties grow and large urban concentrations with major migratory contingents appearing, and is now experiencing development – at perhaps an even faster rate than ever before – which has both a technical and philosophical source.

Our lifestyles have been changed by a sensational growth in the mass media and multiplied the means to live comfortably. Lately we have been witnessing a process of scientific and technological innovation which, in addition to accentuating the social changes experienced, gives mankind a chance to so influence natural phenomena it can even distort and destroy nature which is alarming to any responsible person.

In parallel with these events, a greater lust for possessions is becoming evident, alongside a deterioration in more spiritual and less utilitarian human values, and the primacy of instruction, in the strictest sense of the word, to the detriment of true education. As regards leading a Christian life, the old anticlericalism born of specific historical circumstances, while not having completely disappeared, has generally given way to a less aggressive but culturally more radical, pervasive, irreligious attitude which ridicules, supplants or considers driven by self-interest any door to a spiritual or transcendental world. Many young people are therefore presented with a cultural universe where the hypothesis of God has been excluded.

The growth of means within man's reach, combined with a somewhat obscured conscience as to his spiritual and transcendental purpose and to his deepest sense of existence, opens the way to temptations of self-destruction. The ecological outcry, which has lately become so widespread, is in fact a signal warning of this danger. John Paul II has even referred to the more serious aspects in condemning the 'culture of death', which 'starts with preventing birth (...), goes as far as excluding the disabled and the elderly, to the final solution of euthanasia. Drugs, terrorism, eroticism and other vices also belong to the culture of death.'[11]

---

[11]Allocution to the General Assembly of young people meeting in Rome for the Jubilee, 14 April 1984.

Obviously we are talking about phenomena that are general to the western world. Nevertheless, it seems that, as occurred at the dawn of industrialisation and urban concentration, Catalan culture has seen a faster rate of secularisation – in the positive sense of independence in the temporal world, but also in the negative sense of irreligious attitudes – than other peoples in Spain. This is testified by the tone of literary and artistic publications considered to be representative of modern-day Catalan culture, and the decline of religious practice in circles most closely identified with it.

We therefore invite those who in one way or another produce or transmit culture to consider the responsibility bestowed by the power they hold in their hands. Let us not confuse what may be considered a legitimate complaint about past or present ecclesiastical faults, or protest against specific ways of behaviour, or even some more or less justified resentment, with the systematic silencing or sectarian interpretation of the underlying values that Christianity has handed down and continues to contribute to our culture.

We ask learned Catalans – scientists, writers, artists – to remain open to the constant, sincere dialogue between faith and culture. For their part, theologians are invited to 'continually search for more appropriate ways of putting doctrine across to the men of today, as a repository of faith and its truths is one thing, and the manner it which they are formulated is another'.[12] We encourage all Catholics to work so that the cultural changes we undergo do not lead us to irreligious behaviour and moral decline, in other words, to the old man described by Saint Paul, but to the full betterment of the human being, to the 'new man' in whom 'the image of the justice and sanctity of truth' is renewed (Ephesians 4, 22–24). The defence of man 'for his own sake and no other (...) is the substance of the message of Christ and the Church, despite what critical souls may say on this issue', to quote the words of John Paul II.[13]

---

[12]*Gaudium et spes*, no. 62.
[13]Allocution to UNESCO, 2 June 1980.

The Church in Catalonia

The Christian presence in our land goes back to the very first centuries. The *Acts* by Bishop Fructuso constitute the first documented evidence in the year 259.

With the creation of the Catalan nation, many names linked to the Church also made their presence felt in the newly-formed country. The figure of Abbot Oliva, Bishop of Vic and Abbot of Ripoll and Cuixà and founder of Montserrat, embodies the spirit of a whole age. As the structure of Catalan society began to form, it received the impetus of the Christian spirit through its monasteries and cathedrals which manifested itself in new, decisive institutions such as 'Peace and Truce'. It was an exceptional time, when the foundation of a country and the establishment of the Church went hand in hand. One of the first documents in the Catalan language were the Organyà homilies.

This presence has continued ever since, taking different forms as the years have gone by. The works of la Merced point to a time of plenty. In contrast, Canon Pau Claris, in the seventeenth century, symbolised the defender of the city in difficult times: 'I die, I die discredited, while afflicted Catalonia lives and breathes.'

After 11 September 1714, numerous churchmen suffered persecution for having remained loyal to the institutions of the country and the people's language. These were bad years, but there was no shortage of effort and labour. In 1749, the parish priest of Sant Martí d'Ollers, Baldiri Reixach, published the *Instruccions per l'ensenyança de minyons* (Instructions for Teaching Boys), which ran through seven printings in Catalan. In 1815, Father Josep Pau Ballot published the first modern Catalan grammar book, entitled *Gramàtica i apologia de la llengua catalana* (Grammar and Defence of the Catalan Language). At the dawn of the Renaissance of Catalan culture, Sant Antoni Maria Claret, in addition to preaching always in Catalan as he travelled throughout Catalonia and fighting for its use, published many leaflets and brief treatises in Catalan. His book *Cami dret i segur per arribar al cel* (The Straight and Secure Road to Heaven), was reprinted two hundred times, consisting of several hundred thousand copies.

We then reach Jacint Verdaguer, the genius of a resurgent

language, Morgades, restorer of Ripoll and defender of the catechism in Catalan, Torras i Bages, who contributed to the Catalan renaissance with his Christian reflection on the most decisive thinkers of our history throughout the entire scope of the Catalan language. And the Christians – laymen and clergymen – who played an active role in the recovery of the country's culture, such as Llimona and Gaudí, in art; Maragall, Ruyra, López Picó and Carles Riba, in literature; Cardó, Manyà, Miquel d'Espluges, Clascar and Ubach in thinking and theology; Vidal and Barraquer, Carreras, Carbonell, Father Vallet and his Exercises, Albert Bonet and the *Federació de Joves Cristians* (Federation of Young Christians), Batlle and sculpture, Bofill, Matas and Carrasco i Formiguera, in politics.

We list all these names as an example to remind the reader of the important contributions made to Catalonia by Christians, and to encourage our brothers to keep this contribution alive to the standard of a glorious tradition.

Aside from this exemplary path, we would not want to hide the presence of negative factors, sometimes the result of human weakness, sometimes due to the interplay of acts and reactions which make up our eventful history; attempted orchestration, often successful, of the Church by the temporal powers; interference by foreign ecclesiastic authorities in the national Church, under the guise of politics.

Nonetheless, we wish to state that we recognise and reassert ourselves through this uninterrupted tradition of loyalty to Catalonia, an especially impressive loyalty in the more working class segments of society, and which has sometimes involved unjust alienation and the sacrifice of individuals and institutions. The draconian dismantling of religious organisations, publications and cultural centres suffered by the Catalan Church in 1939, is a relatively recent case of this. A test which, combined with the bloody religious persecution that preceded it in 1936, which should also be borne in mind, was a veritable ordeal for Catalan Catholics.

Pluralism

The birth, history and culture of Catalonia are deeply impregnated with Christianity. Our faith continues alive in very large sectors of our society. Probably there is no other philosophical, religious or political option with the power to summon so many people, even today.

Nevertheless Catalan society is pluralistic, even in religious terms. There are other Christian confessions beside the Catholic Church; there is a large indifferent sector, to varying degrees, with more or less Catholic vestiges and ties; then there are the agnostics; and the atheists. So it is important that we all co-exist in a climate of mutual respect and tolerance.

The Church, in accordance with the principles expressly declared by the Second Vatican Council of religious freedom, a healthy laity and independence from temporal realities, respects the plurality of choice and only asks, as so often repeated over the last few years, to be given the freedom to fulfil its evangelical mission.

From the civil powers, it asks for no privileges, and has no wish to employ any political influence whatsoever or to subordinate their power. As the venerable Torras i Bages wrote over one century ago, 'The Gospel does not have any specific form, yet it can give shape to all of man's social, political and economic conditions (...) the Gospel has immense scope because it is destined to embrace universal humanity in all its forms, conditions and states (...) every social, political or economic form or condition wishes to have exclusive access to the Gospel. The Church expends as much effort in defending itself from its friends as it does from its enemies, because it wants to preserve its independence.'[14]

Taking this view is not a sign of indifference. We are deeply hurt that, using the pretext of modernity and pluralism, many distance themselves from God the Saviour and the Church, thereby cutting off an essential factor of human life. For us this is not progress, but a loss. In fact, the order of creation and of redemption are the fruit of God's love for humanity, who are not called upon to shut themselves off in an inner world, but to participate in the Kingdom of God. The Church, in Catalonia as elsewhere in the world, with full respect for the freedom of all, champions what is spiritually good and, where possible, the material well being of the mother country. It is eager to feed the faith of believers with the bread of evangelical truth and the

---

[14]*L'elevació del poble* (The Elevation of the People), Pastoral letter of 10 December 1905, from The Complete Works, Barcelona, 1948, p. 1057.

sacraments, relying on the help of God to achieve its special mission.

The freedom we demand has its eyes squarely set on spreading the Gospel and we wish to exercise this right fully. The Christian voice should be heard in all sectors of society and not bend under the pressure of those who would like to ignore the fine distinction between the temporal world and the spiritual world, and erase the transcendental choices open to our culture and society.

This is why we especially ask Christian communities not to become passive in their respect for pluralism or flag in their determination to hail the Good News of Jesus everywhere.

Remembering our roots

Catalonia is rich in history and tradition. Our Greco-Roman, Christian, European and Mediterranean roots are the sap that enlivens our collective spirit. It is perhaps because of our turbulent history that historical writing holds such special interest and prestige: these publications always have a wide public readership, far beyond specialised circles. In our examination of the past, we are often searching for the background behind our existence as a people and an explanation for our present.

However, Catalonia is also a land that yearns for modernity and is an open window through which the renewing winds of change and progress have often entered Spain.

Today, as the country opens up to a future ripe with opportunity, with the exercise of democracy and autonomy, and a future that holds such promise, we see remarkable efforts being made to revive celebrations, customs and traditions. However, we often notice something like an attempt to ignore the Christian roots underlying most of these things and even attempts to ridicule certain religious content, playing on the anachronism of some of these old celebrations. How much better it would be to restore the outstanding virtues handed down by our ancestors alongside these popular events.

Canon Carles Cardó, in his examination of the historical development of Catalonia and the rest of Spain, makes a distinction between good and bad traditions, the latter being no less real than the former. All peoples have them. Here are a few examples.

Throughout history, Catalans have been attributed with an

extraordinary love of freedom, independence and democracy. Pau Claris observed – and we have to bear in mind the mentality of the times – that 'men created Kings, Kings did not create men'. In 1626, Narcís Ramon March wrote, 'With all due consideration the inhabitants and settlers of today's Principality of Catalonia are free and cannot be forced to serve His Majesty.' And King Martín exclaimed, 'What other people in the world could be so given to frankness and freedom, or be so liberal as you?'

However, 'parallel to this good tradition, there is also a bad one', wrote Cardó, 'which follows soon after. The spirit of liberty, when not controlled by a demanding moral conscience, degenerates into rebellion and discord, the two defects that invariably appear during bad periods in Catalonia'.[15]

Something similar may be said about the Catalan attitude, 'nearly always ruled by "*seny*" (good sense)', as Vicens i Vives observes, 'and, on certain occasions, by "*rauxa*" (uncontrollable outburst), because it is not easy to understand how, in a few hours (historical time), we can go from a most obscure attachment to the world of minutiae to the unleashing of iconoclastic madness'.[16]

Irony, which sometimes helps a realistic approach, demystification and even straightforwardness, can become self-destructive when it erodes fundamental aspects of collective life, and can restrict spiritual horizons by degenerating into a mockery of the unknown. These too are positive and negative traits in our make-up.

Perhaps one of the most traditionally recognised virtues of the Catalan is his aptitude for hard work, 'the axle of the country's vital drive'.[17] Perhaps social changes over the last few decades have diluted some of the classic features of this spirit, but basically our people have preserved their liking for initiative and creativity, which form the major drive behind industriousness. This basic attitude must always be at the service of not only the individual but the community as a whole, with a united vision and a willingness to serve the less fortunate.

We would especially like to see the Catalan tradition of a united family life, today threatened in so many ways, made more

---

[15]*Les dues tradicions* (The Two Traditions), Barcelona, 1977, p. 87.
[16]*Noticia de Catalunya* (News from Catalonia), second edition, Barcelona, 1960, p. 222.
[17]Vicens i Vives, *Noticia de Catalunya* (News from Catalonia), p. 52.

contemporary and strengthened. We are convinced that making an effort towards conjugal loyalty, harmony across the various generations in the family, introducing children to essential virtues, and an open, generous approach to life, apart from their intrinsic value, would make a positive contribution to the future of our country, seriously affected as it is by the falling birth rate.

Now more than ever before, it is important to keep our eyes peeled to be able to distinguish the wheat from the chaff, good traditions from bad. We should get back in touch with the best of what history has handed down to us and turn it into a force that propels us towards a future of co-habitation, culture and progress, in all their facets.

Social justice

The efforts of our people have generated wealth. Since our entry into the age of industrialism we have become a modern, progressive society. Unfortunately, it has also been accompanied, and continues to be accompanied, by the blemishes of modern society, among them the unjust distribution of wealth and the deplorable living conditions of broad sections of the population.

Today, in times of economic instability and crisis which is most dramatically expressed by the number of unemployed, already some twenty-two per cent of the active population, a spirit of unity is needed more than ever.

Despite its major figures, initiatives, and the promising work carried out by Social Catholicism, shortly to mark its birth some hundred years ago from the *Rerum Novarum* by Leo XIII, it has not managed to gel into a sufficiently vigorous movement that might shake up our society. We have swayed back and forth between progressive minorities, for this very reason perhaps making such little social impact, and majority mediocrity.

Even today we must avoid the dangers of cutting ourselves off from the true social education of our fellow Christians – one based on the Church's teachings, gradually modernised and enriched by the efforts of recent Popes – brought about by the combined action of those who believe that faith should have no influence on their interests and the few who consider Catholic social doctrine to be superfluous.

On the subject of unemployment, on 3 November 1980 the Episcopal Conference of Tarragona published a lengthy, detailed document entitled 'Unemployment, the Scandal and Challenge of Our Times' which analysed causes, consequences and possible ways to solve the problem.

The present Pope has also often spoken of this issue. On 7 November 1982, he came to Montjuïc, Barcelona, during his pastoral visit to our country and addressed workers and business-men in a beautiful, powerful speech. These were his words: 'We need to create, with all the possible means at our disposal, an economy that is at the service of mankind. To overcome conflicts between private and collective interests, to vanquish self-interest in the fight for survival, there must be a true change of attitude, lifestyle and values; there must be a true change of heart, mind and soul: converting man to truth, for the sake of man.'

Certainly, there is no easy answer to the problem of compul-sory unemployment. Something is failing to work in state mechanisms and plans, and something is also amiss in the social behaviour of the people. However, it is important for us all to make an effort, as best we can, taking a highly responsible approach: the authorities, by orienting public resources wher-ever possible towards job creation; businessmen, by bearing in mind not only the most convenient short-term profitability in their investments, but also social interests; and all citizens, by adopting a more demanding ethical attitude towards closed-shop salaried employment and perhaps abusing the unemploy-ment benefit system.

And where the strict fulfilment of civic duties goes no further, then initiatives of compassionate love must reach, by pursuing and supporting the work undertaken by Caritas and other eccle-siastical and lay bodies.

Achieving a fair society, ridding it of ugly contrasts and allow-ing the whole population to feel they are free citizens in this country, must be an objective of the utmost priority in Catalo-nia today. An objective towards which it is essential for all of us – individuals and institutions – to contribute their combined efforts, according to their position.

Those who have arrived from outside

Although the phenomenon of migration has gradually dimin-ished and, by now, the large majority of citizens have been here for at least a few years and exercise their democratic rights, the imprint left by this important phenomenon is perceptible. Especially as regards the degree of understanding and assimilation of the native language and culture.

It is therefore still necessary for us to include in our social duties our cordial, generous welcome to those who have come from other lands to share our life and, for their part, a sense of unity with their new community.

It should be pointed out, as has so often been repeated in recent years, that Catalonia has had a long, prolific tradition of integration. Prime land or a through-route since its beginnings, it has been a melting-pot which has managed to take the *homines undecumque venientes* from the north and the south into its aspirations as a people. 'We are the result of various yeasts,' said Vicens i Vives. Even at a difficult time, when the Catalans had been forced into a defensive position, we find this beautiful line from the famous *Pedra de Toch* (The Touchstone) (1641) 'Catalonia, mother of foreigners'.

An essential part of this idea is the underlying feeling that our nationality is not based on a 'racial factor, a union of blood', but on 'a cultural phenomenon that is capable of binding individuals from the most varied races', as Carles Cardó wrote in 1934.

The work of the Church in this field, especially over the last 25 years, has been more important than is generally believed in public opinion. The extraordinary process of creating new parishes in new, troublesome neighbourhoods on the outskirts of towns and cities, especially in the Barcelona area, has not only been very important pastoral work but has, in addition, proved to be a major social impetus. Over the years schools, housing co-ops, cultural associations and even unions have grown around the original parish churches, which for a long time were the only active presence of Catalan society in immigrant areas. With them, the first ever network of social assistance centres to be seen in the neighbourhoods, were set up with the help of the Caritas organisation. We do not mention this to glorify ourselves but to acknowledge all the laymen, priests and religious devotees who have contributed to making this approach work and keeping it alive.

We ask parish congregations to continue setting an example of co-existence by respecting all cultural traditions, and offering facilities for access to the everyday use of our language, in true Christian brotherhood. Today, our pastoral advice is sought by a large number of Christians who were not born in Catalonia, and we are proud that the ecclesiastical community has been able to set this as a particular example to the rest of the country as a whole.

Epilogue

Before closing this reflection, we must add that we would not like these thoughts on earthly realities to give the impression that we are ignoring our final destiny. Far from forgetting it, we are well aware that our citizenship in the motherland here below is a path, a pilgrimage and in provisional anticipation of a blessed and eternal citizenship in the future.

In all honesty, the two citizenships do not contradict one another, but complement one another. The Christian does not live on Earth to save only himself, ignoring the day-to-day problems of his fellow man, rather he hopes that by exercising his duties as a citizen in the right way he will help his community and others to exercise theirs.

This is expressed by the Second Vatican Council: 'Our hopes for a new Earth should not weaken us, but rather arouse the concern of Christians. Co-operation in the organisation of human society is of great concern to the Kingdom of God. Possessions like human dignity and freedom... we will find once more. The Kingdom of God is already here on Earth'.[18]

Therefore, if the Kingdom of God is already here, we must live as citizens worthy of this Kingdom, illuminated by the Gospel and helped by the Church, and always loyal to God and man.

As a final point, we recite a prayer by Bishop Torras i Bages, the spiritual patriarch of Catalonia, from his well-known *Visita espiritual a la Mare de Deu de Montserrat* (A Spiritual Visit to Our Lady of Montserrat), which we would like to be on the lips and in the hearts of all Catalans: 'Lady of Montserrat, whose holy mountain is encircled by olive trees, the symbol of peace, secure a lasting Christian peace for Catalonia.'

The Bishops of Catalonia
27 December 1985
Feast-day of Saint John the Evangelist

---

[18]*Gaudium et spes*, no. 39.

'The Catalan Problem': The Doctrine of the Church[19]

Further evidence of the teachings of John Paul II is to be found in the homily delivered in the sanctuary of Jasna-Gora. In this homily, the Pope speaks to the Polish people on how unity, of both family and nation, depends on justice and love. Here he does not discuss nationalism within a plurinational state, but principally unity between fellow nationals, and also makes allusion to union between the peoples and nations that form states. The first lesson of the text is that all nations must seek unity on the basis of justice and love. However, the text is very useful for our train of thought when it states, by chance, what constitutes a nation: it is not something from without, as the obsession of one country for another can be, but a factor that surges from within, that is to say, for cultural reasons. Having said that unity is dependent on justice to meet the needs and guarantee the rights and duties of every member of the nation, he adds that one has to make a great effort to overcome the not inconsiderable difficulties that arise when it comes to unity between the children of a common mother country. He then continues with the following thoughts, which fit in perfectly with the concept of nation, mentioned several times elsewhere. He says:

'This effort must go hand in hand with love for one's country, love for its culture and history, love for its particular values which help place the nation within the large family of nations. In short, love for one's fellow nationals, men who speak the same language and are responsible for the common cause called "Mother Country".'

The Pope exhorts us not only to unity but also to reconciliation between nations, the precondition of which is:

'the recognition of and respect for the rights of every nation. Above all, this means the right to existence and self-determination, the

---

[19]In the end I have decided to include this fragment from my other book *El problema catalán* (The Catalan Problem) entitled, The Doctrine of the Church (p. 153-157). Ediciones Encuentro, Madrid, 1994. Although it does not consist of a strictly pastoral document, it represents the thoughts of a bishop who wrote it fully aware that he was a shepherd of the Church.

right to one's own culture and its multifaceted development. We know full well, from the history of our mother country, the cost of infringement, violation and negation of these inalienable rights.'

Naturally enough, the Pope speaks of Poland which is his home-land, a people with a desolate history whose neighbours have not been in the habit of showing much respect towards the rights of the Polish people.

Here I include another important text by Pope John Paul II, which is a fragment of a speech given to the French bishops of Mediterranean Provence on 18 November, 1982:

'I wish to add some further words on the cultural patrimony of your regions, to which religion undoubtedly contributes. It is very important for it to be respected and to insist on this respect. Surely it is impregnated with Christian vitality and spirit? Unfortu-nately, one is often working for a firm that secularises these spiri-tual riches. There is clear, evident correlation between popular culture and the faith of a people. However, to prevent this secu-larisation we need to help and value all men of goodwill, Chris-tians or otherwise, who attempt to preserve this patrimony. Your country is doing much that is praiseworthy in this field, led by teachers, by cultural organisers and artists, by people who strive to preserve or revive regional tongues, even people who produce regional television and radio programmes. In the end it amounts to respect for the Christian context of this patrimony, by nature permanent and always relevant, beyond the vicissitudes of history. The Church should be the first to understand this need, to take an interest, to contribute and to bear witness to it.'

The text is substantial and beautiful, and requires no further commentary. The following text, taken from the allocution by Pope John Paul II to the bishops of French Midi on the last *ad limina* visit, is also relevant:

'In particular, as regards your region of Occitaine or Catalan culture, which has developed its own character and personality, I am well aware of your hopes and fears. For example: the prob-lems of the dispersal of Christians, the visible presence of the Church, the isolation of priests, faith in the young, the right language to use in order to appeal to public opinion... '

Here is also another document, the text of a speech by Pope John Paul II, on his visit to Tokyo, Japan in 1981:

'The culture of every nation is expressed, among other ways, but particularly, by language. Language is the form we give our thoughts. Language embraces the individual traits of a people's and a nation's identity. The heartbeat of the nation, somehow, lies there, for language, one's own language, gives expression to whatever it is that feeds the soul of a community, the family, a nation, history.

'We cannot run away from the great effort it takes to build a just city for sons of the same country. It is an effort which must go hand in hand with love for one's country, love for its culture and history, love for the particular values which determine its place among the great family of nations. In short, love for one's fellow countrymen, men who speak the same language and head the common cause called mother country.'

Finally, from a later document, the speech given by Pope John Paul II to the diplomatic corps on 14 January 1984 – published in *L'Osservatore Romano* on the 15th and in *La Documentation catholique* on the 19th of that same month – entitled 'The Roads of a World Community of Peoples', is highly recommended reading. Numbers 3 and 4 require sitting back at your leisure to ponder their full meaning. The complete quotation would be too long, so I have picked out only the following lines, which are the ones that relate most closely to our subject:

'On the other hand, sovereign countries, whether they have been independent for some time or who have only been so a short time, sometimes see their integrity threatened by the internal opposition of a group that may even go so far as to consider or to request secession. These cases are complex and varied, and each one of them would need to be judged differently according to ethics that bear in mind both the duties of nations, based on the homogenous culture of peoples (cf. my speech to UNESCO, 2 June 1982, no. 15), and the rights of states to their integrity and sovereignty. We hope, beyond impassioned emotions, and avoiding violence at all costs, well-expressed balanced forms of politics are found that can respect characteristic cultural, ethnic and religious features, and, in general, the rights of minorities.'

It is not hard to form a legitimate conclusion from the texts of the Magisterium of the Church, it is none other than what I am attempting to convey in this book. In these official texts, the Magisterium constantly defends small nations, ethnic and national minorities, their cultures and cultural values, especially language, and all their legitimate interests. Clearly what is said of these peoples, whose sum of cultural values is far less remarkable, in many cases, than Catalonia, can be said with more reason, *a fortiori*, about our nation, a people with a rich, prominent cultural and historical personality. Generally, Catalonia has been treated the opposite of how the Magisterium says it should be, because 'Castilian' state nationalism has often acted politically in the same way – and history bears witness – as the states which are disapproved of in the Church document. Catalonia has in abundance what the Pope says constitutes or demonstrates nationality. The Pope, understandably, does not specify what political solution should be offered to peoples whose rights are not respected, in order to see that justice is done. It is obvious, however, that he is demanding that justice should be done as far as it can. It is not the intention of this book, either, to specify a political solution to the Catalan problem – as I have suggested elsewhere – because that does not fall within the scope of the mission or ethical-religious purpose. That is the concern of politics: it is for the fair-minded, realistic and understanding citizens to solve, as much in Catalonia, as in the rest of Spain and the state. This book has been written for the purposes described before elsewhere, and to wake up those who are still slumbering to a certain extent in ignorance or indifference, and to urge those who have prejudices, outdated now, to reflect again and come to terms with real life. We are still faced with a problem which needs to be solved, called the 'Catalan problem', and this problem needs to be solved fairly, not out of charity, but in acknowledgement of a right. The answer can only be found if, in both Catalonia and 'Castile', there is more clarity of vision and thinking and a spirit of genuine willingness, in other words, the right atmosphere and frame of mind. There can be no provisional solution, here today and gone tomorrow, just circumstantial political changes; it must be permanent and stable, the mature result of a profound change in attitude and atmosphere. For a change like this to occur we need to discuss more, to reflect more, to be better informed, to discard old prejudices more and, for Christians, to pay more attention to the Church's teachings.

For the issue under discussion, there is also much significance to be found in the famous International Moral Code of Mechelen, though, of course, not to the same extent as a document of the Magisterium, given its history and authors. From this I offer the following fragment:

'A national minority undoubtedly has the right to subsist embraced by the wider community of which it forms part, and to pursue and preserve its particular culture. The state to which it belongs has a duty to use all in its power to assist it in this purpose. Should the state, under the pretext of safeguarding unity, pursue a brutal policy of levelling and assimilation, it has failed in its mission. Then, if it has no other means available and does not go against the international common good, the separatism of the oppressed nationality may be legitimised.'

APPENDIX TWO

POLITICAL DOCUMENTS

I enclose below a brief anthology of significant writings on certain political decisions which, in the course of history, have affected relations between various central regimes and Catalonia. Some of these have already been quoted in the book, but their inclusion here puts them in another perspective, as parts of a whole.

In the first part, the anthology is comprised of texts opposed to Catalonia as a national, cultural and linguistic reality. The second part consists of texts that are relatively positive in their recognition of Catalonia as a reality.

I have no intention of analysing the documents in depth. However, in the first part I suggest the reader bear in mind the three following facts:

a) 'Reducing to the manner and laws of Castile without difference' involves admitting the prior fact of the plurality of kingdoms (see 1). The Catalan national factor is explicitly recognised by issuing instructions against the Catalan language, in 7. The rejection of the differential factor by the law of the victor appears in 22.

b) Force of arms as a decisive and/or convincing argument appears in 2 (the entry of the King's armed forces), 4 and 6 (to subjugate by force), 7 (military tribunals), 9 (the entry of our glorious armed forces in Catalan territory), 22.

c) As regards cultural, educational and linguistic factors, it is important to be conscious of aspects negating (everything

Catalan) and imposing (official Spanish) in the field of teaching (books, writing and speaking, 5), 8, 10 and 14 (governmental proceedings), 15 (punishment and cautioning of teachers and, in the event of repeated offence, removal from the official Educational Board), 18 (proposal for the expulsion [of teachers] from Catalonia). Additional fields include the theatre (9 and 12), public deeds (11 and 27), mortgage rights (16), the registration of names (20), legal entities (21), shops (24), provincial and municipal corporations (26), publications by the Ministry of Information and Tourism (28), etc.

After 32, the anthology moves from the negative to the positive, in varying degrees: firstly, in the light of the Spanish Constitution, 1978; secondly, in the light of the Statute of Autonomy for Catalonia, 1979; thirdly, in the light of a resolution by the Parliament of Catalonia, 1989.

Texts Opposed to Catalonia as a National, Cultural and Linguistic Reality[1]

1
1621. Advice from the Count-Duke of Olivares to Felipe IV

'May Your Majesty take as the most important matter of His Monarchy the business of becoming King of Spain. By this I mean, Sir, that Your Majesty should not be content with being King of Portugal, of Aragón, of Valencia and Count of Barcelona, but should procure and consider with mature, secret council to reduce these Kingdoms that make up Spain, to the manner and laws of Castile without difference.'

Cánovas del Castillo, *Estudio del reinado de Felipe IV* (A Study of the Kingdom of Felipe IV, part of the Complete Works (Madrid, 1888)), p. 56–60.

2
1714. Dissolution of the Generalitat de Catalunya (Government of Catalonia)

'The representatives of the *Diputació* (Council) and the *Generalitat de Catalunya* (Government of Catalonia) having relinquished their posts due to the entry of the forces of Our Lord the King (Whom God Protects) in this city and square, His Excellency the Marshal Duke of Berwick and Liria has entrusted me to order and command the members of parliament and judges of the General of Catalonia, to remove all insignias, and for them and all their subordinates to relinquish totally the exercise of their responsibilities, employment and offices, and deliver the keys, books and all other affairs concerning said *Diputació* and its departments...'

Decree dissolving the *Generalitat de Catalunya*, announced by José Patiño, president of the *Real Junta Superior de Justicia y Gobierno* (Royal Superior Board of Justice and Governance), in Barcelona, 16 September 1714.

---

[1]See *El llibre negre de Catalunya. De Felip V a l'ABC* (The Black Book of Catalonia. From Felipe V to the ABC), by Josep M. Ainaud de Lasarte. Published by La Campana, 1995.

3
1715. Prohibition of Catalan Books in Schools, Including the Catechism

'That schools shall not allow books in the Catalan tongue, nor allow it to be written or spoken within the school, and that the Christian doctrine shall be and shall be learnt in Castilian...

'With the newly created and elected Chancellery in Catalonia and having the same dependency on the Council as the other Chancelleries, in accordance with the laws of Castile, you will familiarise yourselves with and be treated as Castilians, never to have reason for complaint nor desire for any other government.'

Taken from the report by José Patiño to the 'Conference of the Council of Castile on the New Government to be established in Catalonia', 13 June 1714.

4
1716. Decree Announcing the New Programme

'... My armed forces, with divine assistance and the justice of my cause, having entirely pacified the Principality of Catalonia, it falls upon My Sovereignty to establish government therein ...'

Decree Announcing the New Programme, signed by Felipe V, 16 January 1716.

5
1716. The Prohibition of Catalan in the Administration of Justice

'The pronouncements of the Royal Audience shall be delivered in the Castilian tongue.'

Art. 4 of the Decree Announcing the New Programme, 16 January 1716.

6
1716. The Importance of Standardising the Tongue

'The importance of standardising the tongue has always been

widely recognised, and is a sign of the dominance or superiority of Princes or nations, whether to flatter and please in a show of dependency and adulation, feigning a nature other than their own with similarity of tongue, or to subjugate by force.'

From 'Secret Instructions' transmitted by the prosecutor of the Council of Castile, Don José Rodrigo Villalpando, to the Chief Magistrate of the Principality of Catalonia, 29 January 1716.

7
1716. 'The Effect may be Achieved without Drawing Attention '

'...but as each Nation seems to have been assigned a particular language by Nature, it requires much artfulness to overcome and some time to achieve success, and more so with a Nation such as that of the Catalans which displays a haughty, obstinate spirit and a love for the things of their country. For this reason it would seem particularly advisable for us to issue instructions and rulings that are very restrained and disguised so that the effect may be achieved without drawing attention...'

From 'Secret Instructions' transmitted by the prosecutor of the Council of Castile to the Chief Magistrate of the Principality of Catalonia, 20 January 1716.

8
1768. Catalan Prohibited in Schools

'I finally command that the teaching of reading and writing, Latin and rhetoric shall be generally undertaken in the Castilian tongue, wherever this is not pursued, the respective Courts and Justices shall ensure its due fulfilment, as recommended by My Council to the Dioceses, Universities and Superior Officers for its strict observance, and diligence in spreading the general language of the nation for better harmony and a reciprocal bond.'

Article VII of the Royal Decree signed by Carlos III, in Aranjuez, 23 June 1768.

9
1801. Prohibition of Theatre in Catalan

'In no theatre in Spain shall acting, singing or dancing parts be conducted in any language other than Castilian.'

Instructions for the Regulation of Theatres and Comedy Companies Outside the Court. Madrid, 11 March 1801.

10
1857. Ban on the Catalan Language in Public Schools

'The Grammar and Spelling of the Spanish Academy shall be the sole compulsory text for these subjects in public education.'

Article 88 of the 'Moyano Law' on Public Instruction, 7 September 1857, compulsory for the whole Spanish State.

11
1862. Catalan Forbidden in Public Deeds

'Public instruments shall be drawn up in the Castilian language and be clearly written, without abbreviations or blank spaces.'

Article 25 of the Law on the Profession of Notaries, 28 May 1862.

12
1862. Catalan Theatre, again Prohibited

'In view of the information sent to this Ministry by the acting censor of the Kingdom's theatres dated the 4th instant, remarking on the large number of dramatic productions submitted to the censor board written in different dialects, and bearing in mind that this novelty necessarily influences and fosters their spirit, thereby destroying the most efficient means for the national language to become generalised, the Queen (whom God protects) has seen fit to rule that henceforth no dramatic works shall be admitted to the censor that are written exclusively in any of the dialects of the provinces of Spain.'

Royal Order of 15 January 1867, signed by the Minister of

Governance, Luis Gómez Bravo, of the government of General Narváez.

13
1885. 'Memoranda of Grievances'

'We had civil legislation, embodied in our way of being, and civil legislation resulted in being threatened with extinction by the Parliament of Cadiz, having decreed, in principle, the unification of the Civil Code, and the threat continues to this day and is near, perhaps, to becoming a sad reality. We had penal legislation and procedural law, and these were destroyed on publication of the New Code, based, as is to be expected, on Castilian law. The thirst for uniformity of the constitutional period has proved to be as overwhelming as in the absolutist period. Spain is Castile, and all regional interests are looked upon as hindrances to national unity, to be eradicated by whatever means, no matter how violent.'

Memoranda in Defence of the Moral and Material Interests of Catalonia, commonly known as the 'Memoranda of Grievances' of 1885, presented to King Alfonso XII.

14
1900. Circular by the Governor of Lerida Prohibiting the use of Catalan in Schools

'... have obliged this provincial government to issue the document herein warning teachers in the province that they shall in future abstain from using any language that is not Castilian in their teaching, to this purpose choosing books whose text has been approved by Royal Order, using the Catechism identified by the prelate of the respective dioceses, and employing the Spanish Grammar and Spelling as laid down by the Royal Spanish Academy of Language, and duly inform them that failure to observe the content of this circular shall result in the immediate initiation of governmental disciplinary action to rule on due responsibility for disobedience ...'

Circular no. 667, issued by the Civil Government of the Province of Lerida, 27 March, 1900, signed by the Civil Governor, president of the Provincial Government of Public Education, Don José Martos O'Neale.

15
1902. The Punishment of Teachers who Teach the Catechism or any other Subject in Catalan

'Primary education teachers who teach their pupils the Christian doctrine or any other subject in a language or dialect that is not the Castilian language shall be punished, on the first instance, by a caution from the provincial inspector of primary education, who shall report the event to the sector Ministry; should the teacher repeat the offence, having been cautioned, he shall be removed from the official Education Board, losing all rights recognised by Law.'

Second Article of the Royal Decree of 21 November 1902, signed by King Alfonso XIII and the Minister of Public Education, the Count of Romanones.

16
1915. Catalan Excluded from Mortgage Rights

'Documents not drawn up in the Spanish language may be translated for the purposes of the Registry by the Interpretation of Languages Office or competent civil servants authorised by virtue of international agreements or laws and, where necessary, by a civil notary who shall vouch for the accuracy of the translation.

'Documents made out in Latin and dialects of Spain, or in old scripts or that are unintelligible to the Registrar, shall be accompanied by their translation or an adequate copy by a Chief of the Archivists and Library Corps or by competent civil servants.'

Regulation on Mortgage Law, 5 August 1915.

17
1923. The Military Dictatorship of General Primo de Rivera and Catalonia

'First Article. To be judged by the Military Tribunals, from the date of this Decree: offences against the security and unity of the Fatherland or any attempt to disintegrate, weaken or lower perception of it, whether by the spoken or written word, whether by print or any mechanical or graphical means of advertising and publicity, or by any act or manifestation whatsoever. No other flag may be raised or displayed except the national flag on vessels, buildings, whether state, provincial or municipal, nor any other place, with the sole exception of embassies, consulates, hospitals or schools and other centres belonging to foreign nations.

'Second Article. Any infringement against the provisions laid down in the Law and Decree herein shall be punished as follows: display of any non-national flag, six months arrest and a fine of 500 to 5,000 pesetas for the bearer or owner of the estate, vessel, etc.'

Royal Decree of the Presidency of the Military Directorate, signed in Madrid, 18 September 1923, by King Alfonso XIII and the President of the Military Directorate, Miguel Primo de Rivera y Orbaneja.

18
1924. Teachers Teaching in Catalan are Expelled from Catalonia

'An attempt has been made to show me how difficult it is to use Spanish to teach children who do not understand our language. There are no incontestable reasons whatsoever to support the argument. My convictions on this matter are so strong and unwavering that there are only two options available: either all teachers, without exception, teach in good Spanish with unshakeable patriotic determination, or else, should I not be fully convinced that this is the case, I shall propose that the Military Directorate, which has the power to do so, employ its highest authority, with or without statutes, to transfer the incorrigible offenders wholesale, replacing them immediately with Spanish teachers.'

Declaration by General Juan de Urquía, Civil Governor of Gerona, published in the newspaper *La Veu de Catalunya*, 7 November 1924.

19
1938. Repeal of the Statute of Catalonia

'The National Uprising signified, for the political order of the day, the break with all institutions seen to be negating the values that others were attempting to restore. Clearly, whatever the conception was for future standards of local life, the Statute of Catalonia, conceded with bad timing by the Republic, ceased to be legally valid in Spain as of the eighteenth of July, nineteen-hundred and thirty-six. It would be inopportune, then, to make any statement on this matter. However, the entry of our glorious forces in Catalan territory presents the problem, strictly administrative, of having to deduce the practical consequences of this aggregation. It is therefore important to establish a regime of public law that, in accordance with the principle of the unity of the Fatherland, restores to these provinces the honour of being governed on an equal footing as their sisters in the rest of Spain. Consequently, at the proposal of the Ministry of the Interior and pending a statement from the Council of Ministers, I hereby stipulate: Article 1. The Administration of the State, of the provinces and municipalities in the provinces of Lerida, Tarragona, Barcelona and Gerona shall be governed by the general regulations applied to the other provinces.

'Article 2. Without prejudice to the liquidation of the regime established by the Statute of Catalonia, legislative and executive authority resting with the territories over common law and services ceded to the Catalan region by virtue of the Law of fifteenth September nineteen-hundred and thirty-two are considered reverted to the State.'

Decree-Law repealing the Statute of Catalonia, 5 April 1938, Triumphal Year II. Signed, Francisco Franco.

20
1938. People's Names may not be Registered in Catalan

'One should also single out the unhealthy exacerbation of regionalist sentiment in some provinces as the origin of certain faulty Registry entries, where not only a good number of names are listed in a tongue distinct from the official Spanish Language, they also bear a significance contrary to the unity of the Fatherland (...) Franco's Spain cannot tolerate aggression against the unity of its Language, or the introduction of names that clash with its new political constitution (...) By virtue of this, I hereby stipulate: Article 1. In all instances, where Spaniards are concerned, names shall be set down in Spanish.'

Ministerial Order of 18 May 1938, signed by the Minister of Justice, the Count of Rodenzo.

21
1938. Nor Legal Entities

'It is strictly forbidden to use languages other than Spanish either in titles, registered names, Statutes or Regulations, or in announcements and meetings of Assemblies or Boards of entities dependent on this Ministry.'

Ministerial Order of 21 May 1938, signed by the Minister of Union Action and Organisation, Pedro González Bueno.

22
1939. Differential Factors are Regarded as Terminated

'To those others, who speak of a "differential factor", we serve notice that they have been defeated by force of arms, and that if they wish to be brothers of other Spaniards we shall impose the victor's law, for we as combatants, at the end of the war in Catalonia, regard differential factors as also having terminated once and for all.'

Declarations by Lieutenant Colonel Ricardo Alonso Vega, of the Legion, published in the weekly, *Arriba España*, in Olot, 12 February 1939.

23
1939. Catalan Forbidden in Correspondence

'All correspondence having to pass through the Military Censor, the residents of this locality are informed that, for such purposes, letters should be left at Military Headquarters, unsealed and written in Spanish.'

Edict by the Mayor of Mollet, 22 February 1939.

24
1939. Catalan Forbidden in Shops

'Barcelona City Council took the commendable decision, in complete accordance with the spirit of the National Movement, to concede a period ending 31 July next, by which time manufacturers and traders shall write the names and advertising of their establishments in the official language, after which time it shall be mandatory to fulfil the above obligation, without prejudice to governmental sanctions which may be imposed.'

Circular by General Eliseo Álvarez Arenas, Chief of Occupation Services, published in the Official Journal of the Province of Barcelona, 23 June 1939.

25
1939. Catalan Banished from the Streets

'Despite appeals and facilities announced by the Illustrious City Council of this capital for all manner of inscriptions not written in the national language to be removed from public and private buildings and services, as well as from entities which are in any way in contact with the public, and despite the duly announced warning of sanctions, it is patently clear that there are still visible exceptions, due more to negligence than absurd rebellion. Nevertheless as said order has yet to be met, and Barcelona and its province must provide their residents and national and foreign visitors with the appearance of an intimately Spanish land, as it was in the times of its greatest glorious tradition when the monarchs and immortal founders of the Spanish Empire were pleased to establish their court in this city, I have ruled to set a period ending the fifteenth of this month of September, whereby the remaining red-separatist inscriptions are to be removed and any other language appearing on facades, commercial displays, documentation for public use, inscriptions and signs, as well as all manner of writing, announcements and documents by public and private bodies, associations and foundations of any kind and, obviously, those pertaining to public services, without exception, in the capital or in the province, is to be replaced by texts that have been correctly drafted in the national language ...'

Circular by the Civil Governor of Barcelona, Wenceslao González Oliveros, 6 September 1939.

26
1940. Purge of Civil Servants, Teachers and Schoolmasters both in Public and Private Schools for using Catalan

'First. As from the first of August next, all acting civil servants in the provincial and municipal corporations of this province, whatever their category, who in the course of their duties, inside or outside official buildings, express themselves in a language that is not the official language of the state shall *ipso facto* be dismissed, with no further recourse.

'Second. In the case of civil service staff, heads of departments or proprietors in said corporations pending purgation, the said offence shall determine the outcome of the proceedings, irrespective of its current status, and the immediate dismissal of the transgressor, with no further recourse. In the case of civil servants having passed purgation and conditionally or unconditionally readmitted, the purgation file shall be reopened and, since all purgation conducted up to the present date may be reexamined, this offence shall be considered an additional charge under the corresponding heading and, in consequence, a sanction shall be proposed or the already existing sanction increased, and may result in dismissal in both cases.

'Third. The same criteria shall be applied to acting clerks, proprietors or heads of departments attached to any of the public services of a province, especially teachers and schoolmasters of the state, as well as municipal health inspectors. As regards authorised private teachers and schoolmasters, offenders shall be personally disqualified from exercise of the teaching profession.

'Fourth. No information report – when appraised in accordance with that stipulated above – shall be dismissed for lack of proof, it being sufficient to show indications and, at all times, the frank understanding of the case formed by the instructor and expressed in his conclusions, irrespective of the result of tests conducted.

'Fifth. All agents of Inspection and Surveillance, forces of the Armed Police and Civil Guard, both in the capital and province, shall maximise their zeal and vigilance for the utmost fulfilment of this regulation and submit complaints, together with an affidavit, for which the implementation of evidentiary information is recommended.

'The Authority expects the Presidents of Corporations and public services of all types to offer their most assiduous, selfless and patriotic collaboration, in order to achieve the rapid, efficient re-establishment of the exclusive use of the national language in all acts and relations of public life in this province.'

Circular by the Civil Governor and Provincial Chief of Barcelona, and the president of the Tribunal of Political Responsibilities, Wenceslao González Oliveros, 28 July 1940.

27
1944. Catalan Forbidden in Public Deeds

'Public instruments shall be drafted in the Spanish language.'

Article 148 of the Regulation on the Profession of Notaries, decree of 2 June 1944.

28
1958. No More Articles in Catalan!

'The Ministry of Information and Tourism having drawn our attention to the profusion of texts in Catalan slipping into our publications, creating a serious problem for this organisation as various commercial publications have requested authorisation from them to publish texts in the vernacular language as we have done, which would unquestionably be dangerous to authorise, it is therefore necessary to restrict as far as possible the insertion of these texts, and even ones that we do publish should be carefully examined to prevent easily committed mistakes. I trust you will step up your zeal on this issue, in order to avoid the categorical prohibition of these insertions...'

Letter from the Provincial Inspector of Press and Radio, Julio Delgado Martín, 27 January 1958, addressed to the magazine *Vida Samboyana*.

29
1971. The National Council of the Movement Attacks Certain pro-Catalan Minorities

'The Catalan region has lately seen an intensified pseudo-regionalist atmosphere, with political intentions, which is having an increasingly marked influence and becoming increasingly widespread amongst the youth. Lately, certain political pro-Catalan minorities, made up of religious people and intellectuals, using a variety of means, including the '*Nova Cançó Catalana*' (New Catalan Song), the campaign for Catalan in schools and the large profusion of books edited in Catalan, have done such efficient work that the problem is painting an increasingly worrying picture.'

From the paper on 'The Defence of National Unity' debated in the plenary session of the National Council of the Movement, held between 17 and 23 February 1971.

30
1973, 1975, 1976. Attacks and Arson Attempts on Bookshops and Magazines

1973. 18 April: *Agermanament* magazine, Barcelona. Attack, theft and graffiti. 1 May: Nova Terra publishers, Barcelona. Attack and arson. 8 May: Tres i Quatre bookshop, Valencia. Bomb and arson. 4 July: *El Ciervo* magazine attacked. 6 August: Grán Enciclopèdia Catalana, offices sacked. 11 August: Viceversa bookshop, Barcelona, attack and arson. 17 August: Central del Llibre Català, attack and arson. 25 August: Ausiàs March bookshop, Valencia, Molotov cocktail.

New attacks against the Tres i Quatre bookshop and, the following year, also against the Cap Gros bookshop, Mataró, Distribuidora Enlace, Barcelona, Taüll bookshop, Barcelona, Dau al Set bookshop, Valencia, Dalla, Cinc d'Oros, Documenta, FCE, Francesa, Borinot Ros, Èpsilon, Internacional, El Xot, Arrels and Ona bookshops.

The attacks continued through 1975 and 1976, the most significant being those endured by Librería Pública, in Barcelona; Manantial, in Alicante; La Pau, in Valencia; Xuquart, in Alzira, Libros Mallorca, in Palma de Majorca; Abraxas, in Barcelona; Set i Mig, in Alicante and, on several occasions, Tres i Quatre.

J. M. Soler i Sabaté – Joan Villarroya: *Cronología de la repressió de la llengua i de la literatura catalanes 1936–1975* (A chronology of the repression of the Catalan language and its literature), Barcelona, Curial, 1993.

Texts that are Relatively Positive in their Recognition of Catalonia as a Reality

31
1978. Spain, a Democratic State under the Rule of Law

'Article 1

1. Spain is constituted as a Democratic State under the Rule of Law, which advocates liberty, justice, equality and political pluralism as the highest values of its legal code. 2. National sovereignty resides in the Spanish people, from which the powers of the State emanate. 3. The political form of the Spanish State is the parliamentary Monarchy.'

Article 1 of the Spanish Constitution, approved by Parliament on 31 October 1978.

32
The Right to Autonomy

'Article 2

The Constitution is founded on the indissoluble unity of the Spanish Nation, common and indivisible fatherland of all Spaniards, and recognises and guarantees the right to autonomy of the nationalities and regions that it is composed of and solidarity between them.'

Article 2 of the Spanish Constitution.

33
Spanish and the other Languages of Spain

'Article 3

1. Spanish is the official Spanish language of the State. All Spaniards have the duty to understand it and the right to use it.

2. The other Spanish languages shall also be official in their respective Autonomous Communities, in accordance with their Statutes.

3. The wealth of the distinct linguistic modes of Spain is a cultural heritage which shall be the object of special respect and protection.'

Article 3 of the Spanish Constitution.

34
The Flag of Spain and of the Autonomous Communities

'Article 4

1. The flag of Spain is made up of three horizontal bands, red, yellow and red, the yellow being of double the width of each red one.

2. The Statutes shall be able to recognise the flags and standards of the Autonomous Communities. These shall be used next to the Spanish flag in their public buildings and official acts.'

Article 4 of the Spanish Constitution.

35
1979. The Statute of Catalonia, the Expression of the Collective Identity of Catalonia

'**Preamble**

In the process of retrieving democratic liberties, the people of Catalonia regain their institutions of self-government.

Catalonia, exercising the right to autonomy recognised and guaranteed in the Constitution for the nationalities and regions that compose Spain, manifests its desire to constitute itself into an autonomous community.

At this solemn moment when Catalonia regains its liberty, it is necessary to render homage to all those men and women who have contributed to making it possible.

The Statute herein is the expression of the collective identity of Catalonia and defines its institutions and its relationships with the State, against a background of free solidarity with the other nationalities and regions. This solidarity is the guarantee of the authentic unity between all the peoples of Spain.

The Catalan people proclaim liberty, justice and equality as the highest values of its collective life, and manifest their desire to advance along a path of progress which ensures a dignified quality of life for all those who live and work in Catalonia.

Through the institutions of the *Generalitat*, the collective freedom of Catalonia finds its link with a history of affirmation and respect for peoples. A history which the men and women of Catalonia wish to continue in order to make the construction of an advanced democratic society possible.

True to these principles and in order to make the inalienable right of Catalonia to self-government a reality, the Catalan Parliament proposes, the Constitutional Commission of the Chamber of Deputies accords, the Catalan people confirm and the General Parliament ratify the Statute herein.'

Preamble to the Statute of Autonomy of Catalonia, approved by the Catalan people by referendum on 25 October 1979, and ratified by the Chamber of Deputies and by the Senate, on 29 November and 12 December 1979, respectively.

36
Catalonia, Autonomous Community. Its Demarcations

'Article 1

1. Catalonia, as a nationality and in order to access its self-government, is constituted into an Autonomous Community in accordance with the Constitution and the Statute herein, which is its basic institutional regulation.

2. The *Generalitat* is the institution in which the self-government of Catalonia is politically organised.

3. The powers of the *Generalitat* emanate from the Constitution, the Statute herein and the people.

Article 2

The territory of Catalonia as an autonomous community consists of the counties making up the provinces of Barcelona, Gerona, Lerida and Tarragona, at the moment of enacting the Statute herein.'

Articles 1 and 2 of the Statute of Autonomy of Catalonia.

37
Catalan, the Language of Catalonia and its Official Language alongside Spanish

'Article 3

1. The language of Catalonia is Catalan. 2. Catalan is the official language of Catalonia, as Spanish is also official throughout the Spanish State. 3. The *Generalitat* shall guarantee the normal and official use of both languages, shall adopt the necessary measures to ensure their understanding and shall create the conditions to reach full equality as regards the rights and duties of the citizens of Catalonia. 4. The Aranese idiom shall be taught and be the object of special respect and protection.'

38
The Traditional Flag of Catalonia

'Article 4

The Catalan flag shall be the traditional one of four red bars on a yellow background.'

39
1989. Resolution by the Parliament of Catalonia on the Right of Self-Determination of the Catalan Nation

'The Parliament of Catalonia

1. Solemnly declares that Catalonia forms part of a distinctive national reality within the State, a fact maintained by the Catalan people at all times, as much by its political forces, its cultural and civil institutions, as by the awareness of the majority of its citizens.

2. Manifests that compliance with the institutional legal framework currently in force, the result of the political transition from dictatorship to democracy, does not mean that the Catalan people relinquish their right to self-determination, as established by the principles of international organisations and inferred from the preamble to the Statute of Autonomy of Catalonia or 1979.

3. In consequence, asserts that when it believes it to be opportune and through courses of action envisaged by the self-same institutional code, it may raise the extent of self-government as far as it believes necessary and, in general, adapt regulation of national rights to historical circumstances in the future.'

Non-legislative motion 98/111 of the Parliament of Catalonia, unanimously approved on 12 December 1989.